COSBY

—*on being a parent*

"One of the things you learn when you become a parent is the horrible thought and the reality that your children will *be* your children for life! That's why there's death."

—*on show business*

"You know, it's all because I wanted to be accepted. That's why I tell jokes. I discovered that people would laugh at my jokes, and that meant they *liked* me, they accepted me. It was even better when they started throwing *money*."

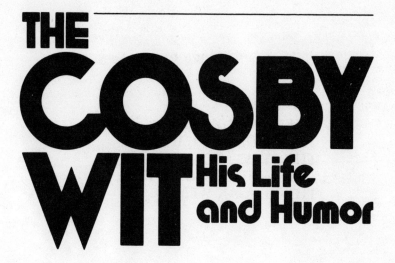

THE COSBY WIT
His Life and Humor

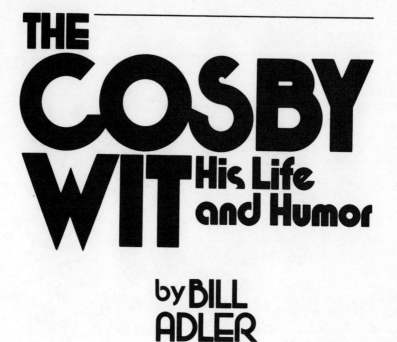

THE COSBY WIT His Life and Humor

by BILL ADLER

Carroll & Graf Publishers, Inc.
New York

Carroll & Graf Publishers, Inc.
260 Fifth Avenue
New York, N.Y. 10001

First printing 1986

Library of Congress Cataloging in Publication Data

Adler, Bill. 1986-
    The Cosby Wit.
    1. Cosby, Bill, 1937-   2. Comedians—United
States—Biography.   I. Title.
PN2287. C632A66 1986   792.7'028'0924 (B) 86-20804
ISBN 0-88184-299-0

TABLE OF CONTENTS

Editor's Note

I have been privileged to work on many books of wit and humor—from John F. Kennedy to Winston Churchill—but perhaps no assignment was more exciting and rewarding than THE COSBY WIT.

Bill Cosby is an American humorist—a great American humorist—like Mark Twain and Will Rogers before him.

He is perhaps *the* American humorist of our time.

In a way, this book is a tribute to Bill Cosby. We have tried to present his humor in an objective fashion but if bias creeps in, it is only because his wit and humor are so remarkable.

This collection was compiled from many sources (a complete bibliography is at the back of the book).

THE COSBY WIT is the mirror of a man who has brought pleasure to millions of people—around the world—and who will hopefully continue to do so for many years to come.

Bill Adler
New York City
1986

PART ONE

PART ONE

CHAPTER ONE

THE LIFE

ALTHOUGH MUCH of the charm of Bill Cosby's humor stems from its unbelievable naturalness—much as if he made it all up right in front of your eyes—the truth of the matter is that he knows exactly what he expects your reaction to be when he delivers a joke or routine and that he has labored hard for the effect he wants to make.

"What I do with humor is to have three levels hitting all at the same time," he once explained. The most important level is, of course, what he calls the "middle" level, "which is the total laughter itself."

But there are two other levels, as he goes on to describe: the levels he calls the "overcurrent," and the "undercurrent."

"For instance, in my monologues, the humor itself goes straight down the middle." The audience identifies with him during his reminiscences and during his anecdotes about children and family life. Total laughter is the result.

A typical "overcurrent," Cosby explains, might be "the fact that rather than trying to bring the races of people together by talking about the differences," he tries to "bring them together by talking about the similarities."

As for the "undercurrent," that is the level, he explains, "that makes an appeal for an understanding of the gap between the ages" in the lives of people.

Serious stuff, indeed, and something Cosby doesn't normally deal with, either in his appearances before the public or in his writings.

Nevertheless, it is a fact that Cosby is actually a man of many perplexing contradictions, just as most people are.

For example:

He is not a race humorist—and yet he *began* his career with racial jokes and routines.

He did not actively support the civil rights movement; indeed he raised the ire of many activists because of his hands-off attitude about it—and yet upon Martin Luther King's death, he made, with his television co-star, Bob Culp, a very high-profile appearance at the funeral.

He has called himself a "frightened atheist"—obviously in jest—and yet of course he makes liberal use of the messages and lessons of the Bible in many of his routines.

In effect, Bill Cosby is a happy mixture of many complex character elements—all of which enable him to create his own brand of special humor that transcends any arbitrary boundaries that might be set up and tends to reach across all dividing lines to bring laughter to all living beings.

How did it all happen? What made this man a symbol of humor and wit and kindness? What went into the making of the essentiality of the Cosby wit?

William Henry Cosby, Jr., was born in a suburb of Philadelphia called Germantown on July 12, 1937, at the height of the Great Depression. His father was a welder who eventually became a mess steward in the navy, and was then away from home most of the time.

"My father is an intelligent man who failed in life," Cosby once said about him. "When I was a child, we kept moving down the economic ladder."

From Germantown in North Philadelphia, called by some people at the time "the Jungle," the family gradually was forced into smaller quarters at the same time the numbers of the family were growing. Finally the Cosbys were relegated to an apartment in a housing project called the Richard Allen Homes—known to the neighborhood as "the projects."

It was here that the family finally settled, and Cosby's father became more and more an absentee parent. It fell to Anna Cosby to keep the family together. There were originally four boys, but James, the second, died when he was six years old, leaving three: Bill, Russell, and Robert. Bill Cosby was the oldest.

Cosby was right about his father; he was an intelligent man. Cosby inherited this characteristic, but for some reason he never seemed to put that intelligence to full scholastic use during his school days. He was constantly being upbraided by his teachers, who knew he could do better.

In the 1940s Cosby's father was pretty much gone for good, and Anna was working full time as a cleaning woman around the Philadelphia area. When Cosby was ten or eleven, he tried his hand at shining shoes. During summer vacation when he was eleven he got a real job at a grocery store, moving boxes and crates around—for eight dollars a week!

There was one grammar-school teacher he had during the sixth grade who made a deep impression on him. Her name was Mary B. Forchic, later Mary Forchic-Nagle. She was in charge of kids who had "problems." Of all the teachers he ever had, she was the one who instilled in Cosby a feeling for education that he never really lost, even though for years he actually did nothing about it.

At the end of Cosby's year with her, she wrote this prescient remark on his report card:

"He would rather be a clown than a student, and he feels it is his mission to amuse his classmates in and out of school."

Nevertheless, at the time he did not alter his ways at all, but continued to go his own way, ignoring his studies and concentrating mostly on "playing." To Cosby, playing was amusing his peers. He had always had a natural talent for mugging and for horsing around, and he made the most of it. To him being appreciated for his humor was tantamount to being loved.

Cosby graduated from grammar school to Central High School, where he went out for football. He didn't really get very far there, though, because he found that the athletic program was full of cliques and that it favored certain people. And Cosby was *not* one of them. Instead, he simply continued to entertain his friends with routines imitating the famous comics of the time: Sid Caesar, Milton Berle, Jack Benny, George Burns.

He was given an intelligence quotient test one day and came out pretty near the top. Soon afterward, he was transferred to Germantown High School and assigned to a class for "gifted students." The tests had borne out what all his friends knew anyway: he was brighter than most of them.

But his gifted peers weren't good companions at all, and he found himself more and more with his friends on the street, cutting up with them and telling jokes and playing tricks on them. It was his grandfather Samuel who suggested to him once, "Why don't you tell the story about you and your brother . . . ?" This more or less set the Cosby pattern.

By the time he had finished the tenth grade he discovered that he didn't know enough to go on to the eleventh. He was forced to go back to take the tenth again.

This was too much. He opted out of school—becoming

an early example of the "drop-out" type familiar to the later generation of the 1960s. Trouble was, he was ten years too early to be a hero in the role, and instead was regarded as a loser.

He joined the Navy, following more or less in his father's footsteps. However, when he recalled it later he saw it in a slightly different light. "I joined the Navy because my buddies had all joined the Air Force and I didn't want to be like everybody else."

It was 1956 and the Korean War was over and the Vietnam War was not yet in sight. Cosby spent his time playing football at Quantico, a marine base in Virginia. After basic training he was assigned as a hospital corpsman to the physical therapy unit at Bethesda Naval Hospital in Maryland. In that unit, he traveled from Newfoundland to Guantanamo Bay.

His four-year stint taught him something very important. "I met a lot of guys in the navy," he recalled later, "who didn't have as much 'upstairs' as I knew I did, yet here they were struggling away for an education. I finally realized I was committing a sin—a *mental* sin."

And so he studied on his own while in the Navy and passed an examination that gave him the equivalent of a high-school diploma.

During his service days Cosby, who had always been called "Shorty" by his peers for obvious reasons—had stretched out into a lean, rugged six-footer. He even won several track and field awards for the navy.

Putting together his high-school diploma and his track awards, Cosby was able to get an athletic scholarship at Temple University when he got out of uniform. He was twenty-three years old, and he was now able to run, to throw a discus and a javelin, jump, and run the 220 low hurdles. He went out for football at Temple, and became a right halfback on the varsity team.

Until he broke a collarbone. Then he was out of it.

To help pay his way through college, Cosby took a job

at night tending bar at the Cellar, a coffeehouse in Philadelphia. He was paid five dollars a night. Cosby had never given up telling jokes and making friends wherever he went. His talents along these lines paid off handsomely in the milieu of the bar. There was a regular comic hired by the management to entertain the guests on a nightly basis, and when the comic was off, Cosby took over for him.

He made plenty of friends. He was a very funny fellow. In tune with the times, he played it racial, and told the same kind of jokes Dick Gregory and Flip Wilson—and all the rest of the black comics did.

If the laugh was slow in coming, he might ad lib at the first tentative snicker: "You'd *better* laugh! I've got a club that's the *opposite* of the Ku Klux Klan!"

During the 1962 college break, Cosby decided to travel up to Greenwich Village in New York, where plenty of the same kind of comedy he was interested in was happening in the night clubs. A Southerner running the Gaslight hired him for sixty dollars a week.

Cosby hardly had the fare to get back to Philadelphia to see his family. He ate lean, he saved his nickels. He watched the other comics to see how they were doing and to latch onto an idea now and then.

But mostly he went back to his own early days for his material. He remembered listening to his mother read him Mark Twain. Twain has become a "controversial" author in the lately enlightened era, but Cosby loved his work. Here was a man who told it like it *really* was. Here was a man who understood people.

There was natural psychology in the scene in which Tom Sawyer got his friends to whitewash the fence for him. And there was a great deal of earthy humor in Huck Finn's conversations with Jim on the raft. Besides, Twain understood and used Biblical situations for the comedy inherent in them.

Twain raided the Bible mercilessly for ideas. In "Noah's

Ark," a section of "About All Kinds of Ships," Twain makes Noah a typical American male, desperately trying to explain to a ship's inspector why the ark should sail.

The inspector's complaint is that the ark is unseaworthy, having no anchor, no rudder, no life preservers, and too small a crew. Noah admits that there are 98,000 animals on board, which would need at least 12,000 keepers!

In "Adam's Soliloquy" Noah relates to Adam the nitty-gritty of the voyage in the ark. With no pump and only one window, "we had to let down a bucket from that and haul [water] up a good fifty feet." Then "we had to carry the water downstairs—fifty feet again."

He says he lost "different breeds of lions, tigers, hyenas, wolves, and so on." They wouldn't drink the sea water with all that salt in it! "But we never lost a locust," Noah points out cheerfully, "nor a grasshopper, nor a weevil, nor a rat, nor a cholera germ."

On the whole, "I think we did very well, everything considered. We were shepherds and farmers; we had never been to sea before." He pauses. "In my opinion, the two trades do not belong together."

Whether or not this particular bit of inspired nonsense stimulated Cosby to do his own Noah thing along the same lines is immaterial. He had obviously caught the classic style of the master, and liked working in the same vein.

In fact, one of his early skits *concerned* Noah and the ark. In time this became *the* Cosby classic. Certainly Noah is Twain's confident American male, just slightly more hip, more street-wise, but practical and no-nonsense, and God is a kind of Twainlike representation of the Supreme Being (with a bit of Cosby's modern-day father image thrown in).

The routine starts at the moment the Lord tells Noah to build the ark. "Noah," God calls, played by Cosby as a deep-voiced echo-chamber persona from another world.

Noah, the hip skeptic: "Who is that?"

"It's the *Lord,* Noah," booms God.

"Right!" Noah responds in solid American street talk. God begins instructing Noah. "I want you to build an ark."

"Ri-ight," says Noah. Pause. "What's an ark?"

"Get some wood," the Lord continues. "Build it three hundred cubits by eighty cubits by forty cubits."

"Ri-ight." Noah plays along. But: "What's a cubit?"

God tells Noah to get two of every living thing and load them onto the ark. Noah: "Who is it, *really?*"

When God explains that he's going to destroy the world and everything not on the ark, Noah sees the light—or thinks he sees the light. "Am I on *Candid Camera?*"

"I'm going to make it rain four thousand days and drown them right out!" says God.

"Ri-ight!" says Noah. "Let it rain for forty days and forty nights and wait for the sewers to back up."

"Ri-ight!" says the Lord, catching up on Noah's speech patterns. So Noah builds the ark and loads it up, but his neighbors laugh at him, and he finally tells the Lord he's through. At that moment the sky darkens, lightning flashes, and thunder booms. It's no shower.

Noah believes: "Okay, Lord. Me and you—*right?*"

Cosby started work on the Noah routine at the Gaslight, but of course it did not come together all at once. It took months and years of patience and work to get it right.

At the Gaslight, Cosby got himself an agent, Roy Silver. Silver and Cosby worked hard after each gig, going back over taped segments of his routines, trying to figure out why the audience had laughed at a joke one time, and had failed to laugh at another time.

By July 1962 Cosby was making $175 a week and had a free room. Roy Silver got him a job in Chicago.

An important decision was facing Cosby. He could not continue his education and continue his job in the entertainment business. It was one or the other. One career had to go.

He dropped out of Temple. It was his second drop-out from school. His mother was desolated by his move. She *knew* he was doing the wrong thing, but all her tears could not bring him back to Temple—not when he *felt* that things were going his way and would open up for him in the nightclubs. And soon.

He was wrong. Success was not immediate. There were many near misses, with talent scouts choosing the wrong act in a club, with Cosby passed over for other comics, with even Silver becoming desperate over the Cosby fortunes.

It was the beginning of the big push in the civil rights movement. Cosby had started out with black-white material, but now he was coming across with a different tone. He was separating himself from the racial stuff he had started out with. He felt he had something to say about the human condition—not just the black condition.

But the public was expecting civil rights jokes. When he died during a routine of straight material, Cosby would have to slip in a black joke just to bring back the audience. He hated it. But he kept fighting to do material that was not oriented to the movement.

He began to get good bookings—in Chicago at the Gate of Horn, in Washington at the Shadows Club and the Shoreham Hotel. And so on.

It was in Washington that he met a nineteen-year-old girl named Camille Hanks. She was a psychology major at the University of Maryland. Her father was a research chemist at Walter Reed Hospital. Camille was really almost a member of the horsy set in Silver Springs.

Needless to say, Camille's family was against her interest in Cosby. They considered show business the haven of ruffians, illiterates, and mediocrities—and worse. When Cosby and Camille became engaged, her parents made them break off the relationship completely.

But eventually the engagement was on again, after Cosby met and talked to Camille's parents. Besides, at the same time things were beginning to happen in the life of the up and coming comedian.

Allan Sherman had made two big hit records of ethnic comedy, and was substituting for Johnny Carson as emcee of *The Tonight Show* on NBC-TV. Cosby had been passed over so many times by talk-show hosts that he barely made the audition after Sherman asked to see him. When he got there, he did a routine that had worked in the Village—one about karate actions. Sherman looked at it and said okay.

In front of a live audience at night, the routine went over big. Cosby was the smash of the show. Quickly Sherman produced a record of Cosby's routines. The record was called *Bill Cosby Is a Very Funny Fellow . . . Right!*—now a classic—and was recorded at the Bitter End in Greenwich Village. It was a hit.

His nightclub dates were soon bringing Cosby in over a thousand dollars a booking. He was in demand more and more. On January 25, 1964, Cosby and Camille were married in Olney, Maryland. They had what might be termed a whirlwind honeymoon—in San Francisco, where Cosby was appearing at the Hungry i, in Los Angeles, where he was booked at the Crescendo, and at Lake Tahoe, where he was playing Harrah's. Life was speeding up it's pace.

Civil rights may have been on the minds of many people in the country, but in the entertainment world it was a time of the cold war and of the thrill of espionage.

In 1962 the first of the James Bond motion pictures, *Dr. No*, came out, and was a hit. *The Man from U.N.C.L.E.* was starting out on television—an obvious, lighthearted rip-off of James Bond, featuring the C.I.A. In 1965 there would be *The Wild Wild West* and *Get Smart*. With spies all the rage, various producers were looking for the best way to exploit the trend.

Sheldon Leonard had already scored as the producer of *The Dick Van Dyke Show,* and was looking around for something that would make it in the spy genre. He was watching a routine done by Bill Cosby on a talk show one night when it occurred to him how nice it would be to get someone like Cosby as a spy, with all that humor and that warmth.

But, no, he thought. It wouldn't work. If only Cosby was white and not—

Suddenly Leonard did a double take. He realized he could be blocking out one of the best ideas he might ever have. He had already cast Robert Culp as the star of a new espionage series he was preparing, a show called *I Spy,* with Culp playing the role of a tennis bum with round-the-world commitments to cover his espionage activities. His partner was tentatively cast as George Raft, or a Raft-type, to play against Culp's youth.

But what about Cosby—to play against Culp *as an equal?*

Leonard sent Carl Reiner to sound out Cosby. Cosby figured his appearance would be a one-shot with comedy overtones. But later on, when he met with Leonard in San Francisco, he learned to his astonishment that Leonard meant him to be a series regular, a side-kick for Culp's Kelly Robinson, international tennis bum. Cosby would be Alexander Scott, C.I.A. agent, with a definite wrinkle: he was a brain, a sophisticate, the "Bond" part of James Bond—a Rhodes Scholar, an athlete, an intellectual, master of seven languages, the Sherlock Holmes with his mass of trivia details to unlock codes and solve puzzles.

What Cosby liked about the character was something else indeed: "The important thing as far as Alexander Scott was concerned, and as far as I'm concerned, was that when somebody punched him, he punched them back!"

From the beginning, Cosby and Culp became fast friends on and off the screen.

"The thing that drew me to Bill the first moment I laid eyes on him," Culp once said, "was that he was the angriest man I ever met."

Part of Cosby's anger was in not knowing how he would be treated. "I deliberately said to them, if you make a joke about my color, then I'm going to make one about *your* color!"

Culp notes: "Bill Cosby, without question, agonized over what kind of a black man, what kind of a black American, he ought to be. But he never showed it to anyone. He has far too much pride to do that." But before the show was through in 1968, Culp goes on, "he found out more about the larger picture, the canvas of being a black American, and I did the same thing about being a white American. And that's the kind of canvas that just stretches to the horizon."

From the beginning of the project, nobody thought things would ever come together. Most discouraged was Sheldon Leonard on the set during the first days of shooting. "He mumbled everything," Leonard said. "He didn't listen to other people's lines, so he didn't react properly."

Indeed Cosby *was* warm, smiling, and charismatic in his own milieu of comedy, but he couldn't play a straight role! He kept reading his lines as if he were alone in front of a camera. Instead of reacting, he was simply reading lines to himself.

Luckily Cosby was a natural actor and a fast study. With the help of Culp, an old pro, and Leonard, Cosby finally got the hang of doing straight acting. Naturally, when the script called for a comic line, he was ready with the best. Gradually he learned the ropes.

But all was not happiness at NBC-TV. The top brass was convinced the show was doomed. Who would accept a black as the equal of a white in a title role?

In the end, the pundits were wrong. The show was a hit from the beginning. By the end of the first year, it was in the top twenty! Cosby won an Emmy for his work in the role of Alexander Scott, embarrassed somewhat at not being able to share it with Robert Culp.

The show debuted over NBC-TV on September 15, 1965, and ran for three years. By then Cosby was a national name, and the records he had made long before were hot sellers. His nightclub appearances sometimes earned him $50,000 a week!

It was not only the making of Cosby; the success of the show was also the opening of the door to black actors and actresses in serious roles—parts that had been restricted to stereotypical characters or walk-on gagsters in the past. It was not lost on some that Cosby had done it without joining the civil rights battle in the early 1960s.

The chemistry between Culp and Cosby should not be overlooked. The two were both young men, both college athletes, both track stars, both intelligent and sophisticated men. They shared a sense of fun, too.

The action for the show was generally shot on location in various foreign lands. There was a minimum of closed-set stuff. Actual houses and buildings were used. In one action sequence, Culp and Cosby were supposed to scale a high wall and run across rooftops, then slide down to the ground again. Naturally, contractual obligations forbade them to make the moves; they were assigned stunt men to double their moves.

When it came time to shoot the scene, Culp and Cosby together decided to do it all the way through *themselves!* And they did so. However, the cameras could not keep up with their action, since they had been shut off to prepare for the doubles. The two knew it but did the stunt themselves just for the hell of it.

This camaraderie between the two men came over glowingly on the screen, and even today the show has plenty of style and integrity, even in the reruns. It is obvious now in looking at *I Spy* that the two of them put a great deal of themselves into it.

Cosby's diction—particularly in the use of the word "wonderfulness" and other favorites of his—infuses the dialogue between the two. In one sequence there's even an in-joke based on an earlier Cosby routine.

In this action the bad guys have let loose poisonous snakes in the agents' hotel room in the middle of the night. As the two heroes peer down from their beds in some dismay at the floor seething with slippery reptiles, Culp glances across at Cosby:

"Wasn't there someone who used to talk about poisonous snakes around the bed?"

Cosby simply shrugs.

The bit, as the cognoscenti were fully aware, referred to an early Cosby routine in which he played his "mom" as she left her child in a crib for the night:

"Now you make sure you don't get out of your crib. We've put over a hundred poisonous snakes around it. If you so much as put a toe out, they'll bite you!"

Fun or not, after three years, it was all over, and *I Spy* closed down.

While the Cosby magic was hot, he was induced to prepare a new series, this one without Culp, and starring himself surrounded with a regular troupe of supporting actors. After much hair-pulling it was decided the Cosby would be Chet Kincaid, a school teacher, and that his problems would be those of teaching kids how to cope with various aspects of life.

The Bill Cosby Show was an ethnically integrated show, with Kincaid a high school track coach—middle-class, professional, educated. It was not a "black" show trying to project the reality of inner-city life; instead it had a broad appeal to as wide an audience as it could get.

Cosby told *TV Guide* what he was trying to do:

"I'm aware that the show will have a negative meaning for people who are really militant about any story with a black person in it—black viewers included. But you can still pick a guy's pocket while he's laughing, and that's what I hope to do."

The show premiered on NBC-TV in September 1969, and continued through August 1971.

Meanwhile, Cosby's personal life had been progressing steadily. Camille and he now owned a huge house in Beverly Hills, and Cosby drove the vehicles commensurate with his rating as a star in his own right. One of his cars was a Lincoln Continental, and later he purchased a big Mercedes-Benz.

It was when he was driving around in the Mercedes that actor Theodore Bikel, an old friend from Cosby's Greenwich Village days in New York, came over for a visit.

"When he saw my Mercedes, he said to me. 'What in hell did the Nazis ever do for you?'

"The very next day I sold the damned car and bought a Chrysler Imperial."

Meanwhile his family was growing. By 1972, the Cosbys had four children: Erika Ranee, born April 8, 1965; Erinne Charlene, born July 23, 1966; Ennis William, born April 15, 1969; and Ensa Camille, born April 8, 1975. Their fifth child, Evin Harrah, would be born in 1977. It is interesting to note that both Erika Ranee and Ensa Camille share the same birthday. How the Cosbys managed to solve *that* problem has not been recorded.

Cosby was still smarting over the fact that he had never finished his college education at Temple University. So was his mother, although Anna had traveled around the world with her now-famous son and his wife, and lived with them in great style. Nevertheless, she and her son both knew the value of education and Cosby knew what he was going to do about it.

He now embarked on a complicated mission: to enter the University of Massachusetts at Amherst and earn a Ph.D. in Education. Although he had never even earned his bachelor's degree at Temple University, having dropped out in his sophomore year, the University of Massachusetts had a flexible program; they admitted him to study under their Ph.D. program under the rationale that he had qualified for admission on the basis of his "life experience."

(Later on, Temple University put together a record of his accomplishments, and translated it into a bachelor of arts degree, so he did indeed eventually graduate from high school and college as well.)

Once in Amherst, the Cosbys became enchanted with the countryside and purchased a 135-year-old home for the amazing sum of $64,000—amazing since the house was nestled on a huge estate of 286 acres. Once they had bought the place and settled down there, Camille went to work and refurbished the entire place, repairing all the things that needed repairing and adding her own touches. She spent about five times as much as the purchase price of the house in order to get it into shape, but when it was finished, it was just the place the two of them had always wanted.

Simultaneously with his work at the University of Massachusetts, Cosby commuted to New York regularly to work on a PBS series that was to become *The Electric Company,* a program aimed at bettering the reading skills of seven- to ten-year-olds. The show continued on for five years, going through the 1976 season.

At the same time, Cosby was also putting together a cartoon series called *Fat Albert and the Cosby Kids* for CBS-TV, a show narrated by Cosby himself and featuring him as Fat Albert and other voices as well. It began in September 1973. In 1979, still going strong, the show was retitled *The New Fat Albert Show.*

Finally, in 1976, it all came together for Cosby and his mother Anna, when he finally achieved the one goal he had considered the most important in his life. He received his Doctor of Education degree from Chancellor

Randolph Bromery of the University of Massachusetts. Although Cosby was the star of the day, his mother, Anna, was there—the one who had always told him, "Education is a must!"

The timing was excellent. In just three months, in the fall of 1976, Cosby was embarking on another series for television. He felt that this one was the most important one he had ever tried. The eight P.M. hour in the evening had been set aside as the "Family Hour" by the networks in an attempt to cut down on the sex and violence in the evening shows. Entertainment slotted for that period would be highly moral, clean, and "good."

ABC-TV made a deal with the newly dubbed Dr. Cosby, a deal that was a perilous and shaky one. Cosby was going to come up with a variety show at a time when he was pitted against the most praiseworthy family show ever to hit television, *The Wonderful World of Disney*, and also against CBS-TV's most important and prestigious show, *60 Minutes*.

In short, it was a fantastic disaster. It was not the stumbling of a giant, it was the great fall into the pit of a giant. The show, *Cos*, premiered on ABC-TV September 19, 1976, and went on for barely a month and a half to October 31, 1976, when it was cancelled. It died in a puff of smoke.

It was Cosby's first real flop. Yet it was enough of a disaster to keep him off the tube for eight years.

During that time, he was working out ideas and trying to get something going. It was not easy. In the entertainment business, it is always the last show that counts—not the successes before it—just the last one itself. And this was a monumental flop.

He compared himself ruefully with Hollywood's all-time great, Jimmy Stewart, who starred in a likewise ill-fated television series that had failed just like *Cos*.

"Jimmy Stewart went down the drain the same as I did playing Mr. Nice Guy," was the way he put it.

But Cosby was used to bad days as well as good days. He began studying the programs on the air. He began thinking about his own persona. He began thinking along the lines of another "family" show—one that could be viewed by a family without anyone flinching. And he began seeing himself on the air again as a family man pretty much like his own home life.

The overall style should be warm, gentle humor—the kind of thing Mark Twain had done so well in his better writings. And so finally Cosby came up with what he wanted to call simply *The Cosby Show.* It would feature a man—Cosby—playing a professional person, married to a wife, who was also a professional person, a couple who had, strangely enough, five children, exactly the number the Cosbys had!

And the man's name would be Heathcliff Huxtable.

Yipes!

In addition to all that, Cosby was serious about this endeavor. At the beginning, he hired Dr. Alvin Poussaint, a psychiatrist at Harvard in whom he had a great deal of faith, to oversee the material that went into the program, making sure what kind of people Heathcliff Huxtable and his wife Clair appeared to be on the air. The idea was to ensure that there were no stereotypes of any kind on the program, especially the kind that tend to hurt.

Dr. Alvin Poussaint once explained the mission assigned him by Cosby in this fashion:

"Bill has been very concerned about image, and he's very, very attuned to the race questions, you know, in the United States, and how discrimination operates. That's something that I have always observed as part of his personality, as part of his interest and part of what he wants to change in American society—the negative images of blacks in the media and in this society in general. And he wants to provide hope and positive images to black children."

In addition, Poussaint said he felt Cosby was trying to

do something for blackness "in terms of expanding the concept of what blackness is."

In spite of all this effort, ABC-TV backed down on the project, possibly remembering the debacle of the *Cos* thing. NBC-TV took a look, but wanted the name "Huxtable" to be changed to "Brown," or something like that. Cosby stuck to his guns.

Also, there was another problem. Cosby wanted to tape the show in New York. New York? The brass didn't like that.

After a lot of monkeying around, NBC-TV reluctantly gave a go-ahead to the project, and *The Cosby Show* premiered September 20, 1984.

It was a hit.

It got eight Emmy nominations for the first season.

It retained its Number One position for the second year.

It rejuvenated NBC-TV and moved it from third place for the first time in years.

It looks as if it's going to be up there at the top for some time to come.

The man who made it all work is Bill Cosby.

You've just gotten a glimpse of this man's life. But that glimpse is mostly of his life as it is viewed in public. What about the *real* Bill Cosby? The man behind the man?

Ever since the night in the late 1960s when I tuned in to watch a television show about espionage and discovered Bill Cosby I have considered him to be one of the most talented exponents of comedy anywhere in the entertainment world. At the time of his debut he was virtually unknown to the mass American audience, and his material was necessarily shaped to project a cleverly fabricated personality on the show *I Spy*. He was black; yet he was the intellectual, the Rhodes Scholar, the master of many languages, and so on. In him the stereotypical black was turned upside down—to effect.

Yet seeing him and enjoying him—how he could *communicate!*— led me, like many other Americans, to read or watch every print or television interview. In these he was not confined to the role he played on television; here he was a genuine American humorist, molded in the classic tradition. And here he showed me evidence of becoming one of the all-time greats. I thought so then. I know so now.

Not only does he laugh at himself and at the foibles of his compatriots, but he sets out a specific line of values and goals in the life of the American psyche and persona. This man *relates* to probably the widest age range of audience of anyone in history—from children to oldsters.

How can he do this? Where did he learn his skills? What did it take to create him?

I simply *had* to determine the truth about Bill Cosby.

I went back and watched miles of videotape. I saw samplings of his television commercials. I read hundreds of pages of transcripts of conversations from talk shows. I pored over yellowed magazine and newspaper clippings from private and public files, studied books and documents of all kinds, including even press-agent handouts, reviews, ads, and posters. None of this activity kept me from my weekly date with Bill Cosby on television in that Number One spot, or from enjoying it as much as I always had.

In all, I covered material spanning more than two decades.

From that—from hundreds of such public sources—I gathered the material that is in this book. I was on the search for a specific magic element that would put Bill Cosby into focus for all time. I was trying to find the "active ingredient."

I found it.

It's in every thought *behind* what he says or does.

There is no way to confine him. He is protean. He is mercurial. Like all geniuses he transcends definition and conformation of any kind.

He is just Bill Cosby.

And *that* is the essentiality of Bill Cosby—here for you to look at, read, and admire. I guarantee that if you are a child, a parent, a single person, a man, a woman, a grandmother, a grandfather, a professor, a football player, an astronaut—

—this man will *communicate* directly to you. Sit back and relax. He's coming right at you now.

PART TWO

PART TWO

CHAPTER TWO

THAT'S ENTERTAINMENT!

BILL COSBY'S two main interests in life have proved to be a desire to entertain his fellow human beings and a desire to teach them how to live. From the beginning it was a matter of choosing the proper path to take.

When Cosby opted in his college days to pursue the bright lights of show business rather than the softer, more muted ways of education, he had never really given up his hope for education.

Communication was his main aim in all his sketches, in all his routines, in all his stories and anecdotes. To communicate, to entertain, to uplift: that became the Cosby standard.

"I feel that in-person contact with people is the most important thing in comedy," he noted in a press release prepared by Capitol Records. "While I'm up on stage, I can actually put myself into the people in the audience and adjust my pace and timing to them. I can get into their heads through their ears and through their eyes. Only through this total communication can I really achieve what I'm trying to do."

That was all well and good, but naturally enough not *everybody* understood what he was trying to do. In his own family, especially, there were serious reservations. Particularly those of his mother.

"A lot of parents want their children to be something—a doctor or a lawyer," Cosby later observed. "I wanted to be a comedian. But what does that mean to people? My mother would always say, 'Oh, he makes a fool of himself and gets paid for it.' "

In spite of his mother's reaction, he knew that there was an excitement in show business that he would have sorely missed if he had not taken it up. The immediate reaction! The laughter! The applause!

He once explained when the genesis of his inspiration for an entertainment career occurred. Whether he made it up or not, it is indicative of the way he felt.

"I remember as a kid sitting in a restaurant, eating a pizza, watching a party of about six people. One of them was going on about something, and the rest of them were laughing so hard the food was falling out of their mouths. It was like a light went on inside my head. I said to myself: *'That's what it's about!'* "

From that moment on, it was show business and all it stood for.

Although his mother had looked on entertainment as a business in which Cosby acted the fool and got money for it, there were times when things turned out just the opposite. He told a crowd at the Apollo Theater in Harlem once that no man in the theater could be arrogant or conceited about himself.

"In show business, you can be rich today and back in the projects tomorrow."

Most of the time he just felt *good* about being a star. After his first fame on television's *I Spy,* he bought a big house in Beverly Hills and drove fancy cars around. It was part of being a prominent personality!

"In Beverly Hills we used to live down the street from Jack Lemmon," he reminisced once on the Phil Donahue show. "Or up the street from Jack Lemmon. And I used to go by Jack Lemmon's house. This was in the sixties."

Camille would ask Cosby, "Why don't you leave that man alone? Why do you keep going down to his house?"

And Cosby told her, "Because he's Jack Lemmon."

"But you keep going by there," Camille insisted. "Why do you go in there?"

Cosby said, "Because it is Jack Lemmon." And he said, "Do you know why he's opening that door?"

Camille shook her head. "Why?"

"Because *I'm* Bill Cosby!"

And inside the house Lemmon was saying, "Look, Bill Cosby's coming by my house."

Cosby told Camille, "I'm going *in* Jack Lemmon's house. Don't you *understand* what it's like to be a star?"

"So," Cosby went on, "Jack and I, we went to Cary Grant's house, and he said, 'Throw both of those bums out of here.' "

As for the fast cars, Cosby sported so many different models that he could look back at a later date and remark casually:

"I bought a Ferrari once, but had to get rid of it because I couldn't find the horn when a bus started to back into me."

There were times when nothing he did professionally suited *anyone*. And he learned a lesson by trying to be all things to all people in the early years of his career. He worked it out as a formula—actually, a nonformula.

"I don't really know the exact formula for success," he told a magazine writer at *Essence,* "just some of the ingredients. It's when you are trying to be everyone's main man, thinking that you are, believing everyone loves you, that you walk into a mess of trouble as an artist and as a person. If I may not know the exact formula for success, I *do* know the exact formula for failure: and that's trying to please everybody."

At times he let it all hang out, as when he appeared on a spring date in 1974 at the Nanuet Theatre-Go-Round just outside New York City in Roseland County. When he arrived at the show, only one quarter of the 3,200 seats were filled. It looked like a disaster area from some nuclear-bomb doomsday movie. Cosby didn't hold anything back.

"I had some opening remarks like 'I'm glad to be here,' but that was before I saw the crowd."

There was dead silence. He looked around, quirked an eyebrow. "Is there a flu epidemic? Are the stores open later?"

Still no reaction. Then, pleadingly: "Give me *some* sort of an out, will you? All the people didn't get back yet from intermission?"

Then a big grin. "Hey, maybe it's a Jewish holiday that's keeping them away. Can they get some group to fill the room, like crippled vets?"

He felt better the night he made the following remark— and you can *believe* it wasn't at Nanuet!

"If I was a youngster wanting to study stand-up comedy, I'd study me!"

Show business gave Cosby friends like Harry Belafonte, Sidney Poitier, Bob Culp, and many others, like Ray Charles. Cosby recalled that one of the most embarrassing moments in his life revolved around a visit to Ray Charles.

"Have you ever been in a position where you were saying something and you *knew* it was dumb? Totally without question, just dumb? And as you got halfway through it, your brain said *dumb, dumb, dumb* . . . but your mouth kept rattling it off?"

Cosby explained how he was invited up to Ray Charles's suite one day. He walked in and found the lights out in the pitch-dark apartment.

"Ray, where are you?" Cosby called out.

"I'm in the bathroom, shaving," Charles answered.

"Ray," Cosby asked, "why are you shaving in the dark?"

Cosby did a double-take in the middle of the sentence.

"I tried to stop my mouth right there, but the rest of it came out anyway:"

"With the lights out?"

Cosby commented: "Dumb! Dumb! Dumb!"

Ray Charles was nice about it. "I've been shaving in the dark all my life," he told Cosby.

Cosby tried to cover. "Aw, I was just joking, Ray. Bet you have a low electric bill, though, don't you?"

Like most artists, Cosby is always "on." That is, by now it has become second nature to be a comedian, even in what is humorously called "real life." One night recently, just after the filming of his current hot hit, *The Cosby Show,* in Brooklyn, he was relaxing at a table in the corner of a Greenwich Village coffee shop, all alone. A waiter came out of the back, turned slightly, spotted Cosby, recognized him instantly, did a startled double take at seeing a big-time show biz celeb, and dumped all the dishes on the tray onto the floor in a thundering crash.

Cosby looked up at him and said instantly, "That's not funny. Now do it again, and make it *funny!*"

Like all entertainers, Cosby has had to contend with obstreperous patrons, especially in the nightclubs where he began his career. He told a New York *Daily News* reporter once that inebriates didn't ever upset him.

"Drunks? No, they don't bother me when I play clubs. It's just that I get upset seeing my fans in an awkward position."

Television, Cosby points out, is a lot different from the theater and the nightclub circuit. Because of the nature of the beast, most producers want to play it safe.

"When I was doing the show *I Spy,*" he said on a segment of the *MacNeil-Lehrer Report,* "Bob Culp and I ad-libbed a line to the effect that some guy was crazy. The censor came in and said we couldn't do that. We couldn't call the other guy 'crazy.' "

Culp and Cosby both thought the line a very harmless one, not offensive in the least.

"Why shouldn't we call him 'crazy'?" Cosby finally asked.

"Well, if you do that, you'll offend all the crazy people."

Cosby actually started out as a part-comedian part-musician, playing drums.

"Once I wanted to be a jazz musician, because those cats got all the chicks," was the way he put it. "So I did a job as a drummer in some joint in Philadelphia. We did four shows a night, and the chicks were there, all right.

"But by the time I finished packing up all the drums and traps, those other guys, with just a clarinet or a guitar to pack away, had gone off with the girls!"

Even years after giving up his drumming, Cosby considered himself quite the performer. In *Down Beat* he wrote: "I was recently playing a gig one night in a club that John Lewis, the drummer, used to run. He introduced me to the audience, and I stood up, and he said, 'You know, Bill Cosby used to play drums. Let's see if we can get him up here to play.'

"So I went up. There were about four musicians, a rhythm section and a horn—I don't remember the guys. We got into a medium-tempo blues, and during the intro, Philly Joe came in and sat down."

Philly Joe was a noted musician and something of a hero to Cosby. So Cosby started to play with *a great deal* of inspiration. "I did everything that I wanted to do," Cosby bragged. The number ended, and Cosby sat there entranced.

"I had really played about as hip a song as I had ever played—I had triplets and *everything* workin'. So, feeling good about myself, I went over and I sat down."

Philly Joe came up to him. "Bill," he said. "You know what?"

"What?" said Cosby, expecting big compliments.

Philly Joe said, "If you take me on the road with you for about three months, I could clean all that up for you."

Except for a few years during his early career, Bill

Cosby never traveled with a huge group of sycophants and hangers-on. He mostly traveled light, and does to this day. When Louie Robinson, a magazine writer, asked him once why he did not encourage such an entourage of friends, camp followers, assorted assistants, secretaries, and valets, Cosby picked up on "valets" and responded: "My mother worked very hard to teach me how to dress *myself*."

Cosby now lives in the East and visits Hollywood only when he has to for business reasons and to see personal friends. He has very definite thoughts about the Hollywood scene, particularly the Oscar Awards, which he expressed on PBS television:

"Viewing the Oscars, I think that the movie industry is no longer absolutely what it used to be. In the old days when you and I were in our teens, studios controlled the actors. The publicity went out *controlled*. We didn't see Edward G. Robinson except on film. We didn't see Irene Dunne except on film. And just to *see* those people alive and see them ride up in their limousines!

"These days everybody rides in a block-long limousine and everybody arrives at some show or other in front of people and everybody is a star. When you look at all the other shows, whether it be the country-western awards, or black music awards, people get to see them more, so it isn't really a *big thing* anymore. The Oscars are still big because the movie industry is big. However, there's no need anymore to tune in and worry about who won an Oscar."

That brought him back to the latest Oscar controversy over the presentation of black stereotypes in *The Color Purple*.

"I feel *that* controversy is one of the silliest controversies ever made up. I saw a television movie with Farrah Fawcett Majors. In it her husband beat her up every two minutes, and then *she* set *him* on fire. Now why is *The Color Purple* such a big thing?"

In the early 1980s Cosby and his good friend, Sammy Davis, Jr., joined forces and produced a show on Broadway titled—what else?—*Sammy and Cos.*

It—well—it simply didn't make the grade. Later, discussing it with Johnny Carson on the *Tonight* show, the dialogue went like this:

COSBY: We went to Broadway and we *bombed*. We had about seventeen people sitting there, man.

CARSON: How do you explain that?

COSBY: Well, it was Sammy's fault. He wasn't drawing at all. *My* people were there.

CARSON: Maybe they just weren't used to seeing two performers on a legitimate stage.

COSBY: Maybe they just weren't—*interested*.

Sammy and Cos wasn't the only disaster. In 1976 Cosby switched to ABC-TV with a show titled simply *Cos*. It too bombed. Cosby was lucky enough to bounce back with a contract to make a movie called *Sitting Pretty*. In one of the interviews to promote the movie he was asked if he thought working in the movies would eliminate him from television for awhile.

Cosby grinned. "I think it was my ratings on my last show that had *already* eliminated me."

Still, with all his ups and downs in show business, Cosby always seems to bounce back, allowing him to make remarks like this:

"I was once able to live in Beverly Hills, for which I am grateful, and then I was able not to, for which I am equally grateful. Actually, I'm grateful for having seen an awful lot, for having done even more, and throughout, for having managed to keep a hold on myself. I've made my choices. Some people need to hang on to Beverly Hills. I didn't."

There is also a sense of awe in Bill Cosby about himself and about the business he is in; an awe that causes him sometimes to cry out: "Up there on the stage—*that's* really me!"

Along with awe, however, also comes a sense of balance. Cosby is a man of intelligence and subtlety. That is what allows him to see his work in this way:

"I used to want to destroy people with laughter. I wanted to make their stomachs hurt. But that isn't fair. It really hurts and it makes people tired. So now I pace myself. I don't want people concentrating on their pain rather than on their laughter."

Show business as practiced by Bill Cosby extends out over the usual lines and parameters of the theater. It crosses over into the specialized territory of advertising. Cosby has been criticized for making commercials and for doing advertising.

A *Newsweek* reporter once asked him why he bothered to make television commercials.

There was, to Cosby, a very simple reason.

"I'm a damned fine pitch man."

He is also a damned fine pantomimist and speaker. But more important than pantomime and speaking is his ability to make strange sounds, combining his lips, tongue, teeth, and hands for the damndest things you ever heard.

One of his recollections that exemplifies this ability was about playing cops and robbers when he was a kid.

"We used to play guns when I was a kid," he recalled. "There were two sounds you could make when you shot a guy: there was *PKHHHH!* and then there was *DHARF* (that's a retarded *PKHHH!*). I put a Band-Aid around the tip of my finger and I went *THUPH!*"

And that, he explained, was the sound of a silenced gun!

In the many years of his career, Cosby has had a chance to study audiences in a thoroughgoing fashion. He has come up with a number of conclusions, among them this interesting point:

"What you fear most is an audience of old people. I

think we all turn more bitter the closer we come to our own death. Old people are toughest because you don't know how close to death they are upstairs."

He has also had a chance to study other careers and other entertainers, coming to this assessment of a lifetime in entertainment:

"I know it's hard to keep pushing yourself into different areas of show business, but you have to if you want to be around in a few years. In this business if you stand still you disappear."

As for his own appearance on television:

"I'd be upset if I looked like a dodo on that TV screen. But I've got no great artistic ambition. What show business mainly means to me is cash."

Leading to one final point Cosby once said to an *Ebony* magazine writer: "A lot of people in show business leave off the word *business*."

Between the years 1971 and 1983, Bill Cosby made nine motion pictures, one a solo feature, written and directed by Cosby himself, the others starring him or featuring him in a segment.

Man and Boy, begun in 1971 and released in 1972, was, oddly enough, a Western—depicting the plight of the black on the wild frontier. A low-budget affair, it had a "modest" showing at the box office that prevented it from failing altogether.

Hickey and Boggs (1972) starred Cosby as Hickey and his old sidekick Robert Culp as Boggs. A detective caper, the picture seemed to be not quite violent enough for its competition—*Dirty Harry* and *The Godfather* (both box-office smashes)—and not quite special enough for an enduring drama.

In 1974 Cosby teamed up with Sidney Poitier in *Uptown Saturday Night*, with Poitier and Cosby as a team of amateur detectives working to retrieve valuables grabbed by muggers. It was a resounding hit—good for teenagers because of its hip action and good enough for the average audience. The critics approved of Cosby's acting job.

Let's Do It Again (1975) teamed Cosby and Poitier against a group of slick con men and swindlers as the two tried to escape the toils of the mob after a scheme to raise money to build a lodge went sour. Again Cosby got good acting reviews.

Mother, Jugs and Speed (1976) teamed Cosby with Raquel Welch ("Jugs"—who else?) and Larry Hagman, before his big-time *Dallas* days, plus others. This one did poorly at the box office and with the critics.

Poitier teamed with Cosby in *A Piece of the Action*, released in 1977, featuring a pair of "lovable crooks" embroiled in a battle with a real heavy—James Earl Jones. Generally, Cosby's reviews were better than the films themselves.

In 1978 Cosby joined Richard Pryor in the high-budget film of Neil Simon's *California Suite*. Cosby held his own against such superstars as Alan Alda, Jane Fonda, Walter Matthau, Maggie Smith, and Michael Caine—but the reviews were mixed. Some, downright hostile.

The Devil and Max Devlin starred Cosby as Barney Satan opposite Elliott Gould as Max. Released in 1981, it was his eighth movie, did ho-hum business, and failed to please the critics *or* the fans.

In 1983 he produced, wrote, starred in, and directed *Bill Cosby Himself*, a solo performance.

In show business it is sometimes the impressions a performer's peers have of him that mean more than his image as perceived by the public looking on from the outside.

Sammy Davis, Jr., who co-starred with Cosby on Broadway in *Sammy and Cos*, told of Cosby's loyalty: "Bill still hangs around with the guys he ran trackw ith at Temple. His friends are his friends are his friends."

Phylicia Ayers-Allen Rashad, his co-star on NBC-TV's top-rated *The Cosby Show*, put it this way: "He's adorable! He really goes out of his way to make people comfortable.

But he's a very subtle man and he sees past the veil that many people wear. He may play around and joke, but when he needs to be serious he is serious. Mr. Cosby is one of the most intelligent people I have ever known."

Mel Gussow of the *New York Times* wrote about Cosby in February 1986, "He is a witty American humorist at the top of his form and in complete touch with the source of his material: himself."

Eartha Kitt, the marvelous and glamorous singer and actress, played with him in an *I Spy* episode. "It usually takes an artist at least fifteen years to become as relaxed as he is naturally. He's fine to work with."

Holmes Hendricksen, vice president of the Harrah organization, said Cosby frequently turned down other higher-paying jobs to perform for Harrah. There was a $200,000 check the late William Harrah presented to Cosby when he was having trouble with the IRS some years back. Hendricksen: "He [Bill] just tells me, 'Look, you guys hung with me when I wasn't so hot, so now it's payback time.' "

Brandon Tartikoff, president of NBC entertainment, put it in focus this way: "Billy Cosby is not just the biggest star in television. He's become the biggest star in America."

Closer to home, his brother Robert once recalled: "Bill could turn painful situations around and make them funny. You laughed to keep from crying."

Critic John Leonard has written: "Tirelessly, Cosby reassures. Love goes on, even if it's black. Children get his message, especially if they're white. Cosby isn't dangerous, in the way that Pryor and Eddie Murphy are, with their secret thoughts and seethings. Cosby bears no resentment; he won't hurt; he affirms; he's adorable."

CHAPTER THREE

CAMILLE

EVEN THOUGH Bill Cosby portrays a man on television with a wife and family very similar to the wife and family he himself has, he rarely brings his real wife, Camille, into his public life as a part of his entertainment persona.

When he does, the things he says about her are surprisingly traditional and tender.

"You know what makes Camille great?" he asked during one interview. "She's incredible looking on the outside, but she's even *more* beautiful on the inside. And that's what's important. I wish a Camille on every husband."

Or, he might switch that around a little bit and reflect on his own good luck in marriage:

"My life is a very, very happy one. It's a happiness of being connected, of knowing that there is someone I can trust completely, and that the one I trust is the one I love. I also know that the one *she* loves is definitely the one she can trust."

There is love here—*and* there is a kind of equality that is hard to achieve in this life. The Cosbys seem to have achieved that, along with a kind of staying power that is unusual in a show-business environment.

Cosby once wrote a magazine article and wound it up with a short anecdote that featured Camille:

"Last year my wife Camille and I finally found a summer camp that would accept our five children. We were supposed to mail the check, but instead we drove the check over, accompanied by a lawyer and a notary public."

Cosby then went on to explain that in order to be *sure* that the kids did get to that camp the two of them had hired a "backup bus" in case of a no-show on the part of the summer camp people and/or bus.

Anyway, the bus did make it and loaded all the children on. "We watched it disappear," Cosby wrote, "and finally we walked back onto our property and headed toward the house."

He then reported that something odd happened.

"We could *hear* our property. We had never heard our property before. We noticed that the birds were coming back. My wife's face began to twitch and tremble."

Immediately solicitous, Cosby asked Camille what was troubling her. "Dear, are you having a stroke?"

Camille answered serenely, "No, I think I'm going to smile."

"What do you think it is?" Cosby whispered in awe.

And Camille said simply: "Peace of mind!"

Although Cosby rarely discusses Camille in any of his routines, he frequently does talk about her in front of reporters and journalists in search of stories.

"This is Camille," he told a *Life* reporter in 1969. And then he went into one of his distinctive imitations:

"Come into the new sauna bath," he invites her.

She does so. "I ask her what she thinks of it," he goes on. And she answers him immediately.

"It's hot in here."

Cosby pauses and looks at the reporter.

"And she splits, man!"

Cosby's wife Camille and his mother Anna were present at the time, and, according to the *Life* writer, Camille immediately giggled: "Oh, Bill!"

And Anna, his mother, chuckled: "That boy!"

Recently, Cosby appointed Camille as the producer of one of his records. This became the subject of a discussion on the Phil Donahue show.

"Camille is my producer," Cosby explained to his host and the audience, "because I decided that she knew my humor better than anybody else, except that she doesn't really know how to play the *part* of producer yet. She feels cheated."

Donahue asked Cosby what he meant by being "cheated."

Cosby explained that she was unfamiliar with the entertainment world. "She's the producer, you know, and when your producer comes to you and tells you how to do something, you say, 'I don't feel like doing it that way.'

"The producer says, 'Do it this way.'

"And you say, 'Take a walk,' and the producer takes a walk."

Donahue laughed and nodded.

Cosby continued explaining how he did that to Camille, and she immediately came back at him with a cry of anguish:

"I'm your wife!"

Cosby corrected her. "No, no, you're the *producer.*"

But she wouldn't have it that way. "No, no, I'm your *wife!*"

"Well, of course," Cosby sighed, "you can't argue with your wife. I told her that. 'You're my wife and I can't argue with my wife. Just do what I tell you.' "

But she refused to do it the way he wanted.

Why not?

"Well, I'm your wife, and you can't tell *me* what to do."

Cosby shrugged helplessly. "So that's the end of it."

And it was.

Camille worked her own brand of one-upsmanship on Cosby over his reputation for being a "workaholic"

—someone who doesn't do anything but work, work, work.

"Everybody calls you a workaholic," she told him once while they were on vacation at Lake Tahoe.

Cosby agreed with her. "Yeah."

She said, "Yet we're on vacation here for six weeks and you told your secretary if anybody called and mentioned work or thought about coming to work that the whole staff would be fired."

"Yeah."

"But I've not seen you in four weeks pick up that phone to talk to *anyone*."

"Yeah."

"I've checked the phone bills and the hotel bills and I know you've not made a long-distance phone call in all that time."

"Yeah."

And Camille said, "I know what it is. You work all the time, yes, but it's not workaholism—it's *greed!*"

Another discussion about love and marriage involved his thoughts on Camille. He was talking to Todd Klein, who later wrote a piece for the *Saturday Evening Post*.

"If you really love each other, then you can make up for your faults," Cosby said. "I don't think anybody's perfect. And I think one of the realities after years of marriage is that whatever changes you had planned to make in that person are going to happen slowly or not happen at all. But the important thing is—do you really love that person?

"My wife, Camille, and I are enjoying each other more and more, mostly because in the past eight or nine years, I've given up all of myself to her."

Cosby thought about that for a moment, and then said quickly, "Of course, if you can't *stand* each other—get out."

On a recent television interview with Gary Collins, Cosby was thinking about his relationship with Camille.

"Camille is not to be thought of as some woman who is tender and kind and gentle and has put up with this guy—me—until he came around. Nor is she to be thought of as some woman *behind* this quote well-known unquote man.

"My wife is so far out ahead of me that I was constantly begging her to really love me. And then there came a time when I did finally catch up—the happiest moment in my life, you see."

And later, during the same conversation, Cosby said, "The greatest thing about love is that when it's there, you know it."

There are, Cosby feels, a few stages of the "children" phase to look forward to. "Once they're out of the house, and it's just Camille and silence. And we go anyplace we want to, and we don't have to worry about anything. I think that's the fun of it, and the excitement of getting them out before you're so old you don't know if they've gone."

He once told Muriel Davidson in *Good Housekeeping*, "I don't need stuff like pot or booze. My high is my wife and kids."

But Cosby is like a lot of other husbands. Camille took him to the ballet one night. "I fell asleep. She says I have no couth and I don't care."

And to Phil Donahue he confessed:

"Camille I love so much that I wish for her a perfect Bill Cosby. . . . Not so much because of what she gave, but because of what I missed."

According to Audrey Edwards in a *Ladies Home Journal* article Cosby said, "More than anything, I know how happy I am at home. In the past eight or nine years, I've given up all of myself to my wife. I'm no longer holding anything back. I find myself falling deeper and deeper in love with her."

CHAPTER FOUR

THE FAMILY

BILL COSBY'S true family life—*his* family rather than his *parents'* family—had begun with his marriage to Camille Cosby in January 1964. It had continued in an unsettled and peripatetic fashion because of the exigencies of the entertainment business. Yet the couple had eventually managed to establish a somewhat shaky home base in Philadelphia at the old Cosby place.

With Cosby on the road it was up to Camille to keep the home fires burning. The situation was far from perfect. Yet the marriage was a happy one and it endured and strengthened without disruption.

When Cosby signed the contract to appear in the television series *I Spy* in 1965, the Cosbys moved out to the West Coast—Cosby and Camille and Anna Cosby included—and settled down there in the sunshine and suntan-lotion belt.

After camping out in a few apartments, they finally found a Spanish-type house commensurate with Cosby's new professional status. It was there actually that the Bill Cosby Jr. family began to grow.

Erika was the first addition, and when Cosby began his stint with Culp on *I Spy* the entire family—Erika, her mother Camille, and her grandmother Anna—traveled with the cast to the Orient to shoot the show on location.

In the spring of 1966, Camille's situation suddenly demanded a change of scenery. Pregnant, she and Anna and Erika flew back to the West Coast, where Erinne was born in July. Cosby had once naively stated, "I thought kids were the simplest little creatures in the world." Now he added a simple afterthought: "That was before I had any of my own."

He began to think twice about children before uttering any statement concerning them, sounding more like a typically harassed father than he had as a single man and entertainer. In an interview with JoAnne Stang in *Good Housekeeping,* he told what it was like on location overseas with *two* offspring to contend with.

"I have four women traveling with me," he told Stang. "You can imagine what happens to the closets when we move into a hotel. I end up giving my clothes to the wardrobe man. There was a time when I was first married when I'd go into the bathroom and find nylons and girdles hanging all over the place, and I'd have to take them all down before I could wash. Now there are diapers and rubber pants, booties, and little woolen hats. It takes me two days to get a shower. What's more, those babies don't even appreciate me! Erika particularly. She has this habit of creeping up in the morning and hitting me over the head with an ashtray. Then she laughs and laughs. Very funny!"

Of course, he assured her, it wasn't all slapstick and comedy.

"I do like taking her out for walks, though. It's great when people admire your child."

Later on, when he was back in the States, he discussed some of his latest observations about the dining habits and proclivities of young children with Johna Blinn, the cooking columnist on *Newsday.*

"Did you ever watch a one-year-old eat?" he asked

Blinn. "They never put the food in their mouths, but stuff the string beans or peas into their ears or nose. Any cook knows that the mashed potatoes have to be just the right temperature before it can be mashed into the hair.

"No kid that age drinks her milk, either. She just spills it down her front.

"And then there's always the dropping game, but you can beat that. You have only to fasten a rubber band on the cup handle and wrap it around the child's wrist. That way the kid digs the rubber band and has all the fun of dropping the cup too.

"Every kid that age is basically a baller. They roll all their food into a ball. That's why it's so important for any parent who's hip to make the mashed potatoes thick enough to mix well with the chopped spinach."

Cosby recalled that even his own mother used to try to trick him by sneaking extras into his breakfast food—to pretend it *wasn't* lumpy. How devious could you get?

"The lumps were always there," Cosby sighed, "even though she tried to hide them by putting raisins in the cereal. But I could always tell a lump from a raisin. She even tried putting raisins in my mashed potatoes to keep me from finding the lumps!"

Kids! He was beginning to recognize what made them tick—*really*. It was different looking at them from the level of a parent rather than from the level of a peer.

And yet he was never mawkish about his attitude toward them. He saw that they could be marvelous and yet at the same time essentially mean, selfish, and self-centered. He knew they could do horrible things to one another— and to you!

On one of those insomniac talk shows that is broadcast during the wee small hours of the morning, Cosby recently looked back to the days when he was watching and helping his children grow up:

"When I was a kid and always in combat with my father, I thought there was something wrong with him, and I was sane. But you know, I've lied to myself about how I would be hip when *I* became a father, how I would have compassion, how I would be able to handle situations. You really don't know how tough kids can be— your kids. Anybody without a child, or anybody without *your* child, will be very happy to calmly look at you and say: 'The kid will be all right. The kid will be all right.'

"But as a parent, you keep saying, 'No. The kid won't. That's why I've got to stay on him. I've got to stay on her. I've got to make sure. I've got to check.'

"That's why mothers get up in the middle of the night and call a thirty-five-year-old son, or a thirty-five-year-old daughter.

"So. It's love. It's respect. It's an ego that we are protecting, because they are ours. We made them. And we can't *believe* that they're doing this to us!"

Cosby was beginning to think about behavior and discipline and about how to instill a sense of responsibility into his children—not an easy task, as he was discovering.

"Your children will be your children for the rest of your life," Cosby said on a recent television show. "Now, it's a matter of whether or not you are going to deal with them or not deal with them when they disobey. Are you going to say something, or just forget it?

"I do know that other things on the face of this earth that have children—mother elephants, robin redbreasts, and so on—*leave* them. We're the only ones that allow our children to keep coming back.

"There's one thing we can do. Learn from the animals. There are some things on the earth that *eat their children.* So if you have seven kids, and they're all misbehaving, *eat one*! Just bet yourself that the other six will get into line!"

Huh? *Eat* one? But if you think about it. . . .

Cosby was once asked by a member of the audience at a Phil Donahue show if he had a favorite child, and he said, "Of course!"

"Which one is that?"

"The last one."

Donahue prompted him: "Because . . . ?"

"Because it is the last one," Cosby said.

In spite of all that, kids were kids—lovable, incredible, and marvelous. They just needed a particular kind of attention. Let Cosby tell it, as he did to a magazine writer quite recently: Regardless of race or social status, parents perceive themselves as people who work hard and have wisdom to hand down to their children," he said. "And they all see their children as these *brain-damaged* people who repel wisdom.

"When I first became a parent, I had certain ideas about how I was going to control the children, and they all boiled down to this: Children just need love."

Cosby paused to let that thought—highly sophisticated and at the same time quite simple in concept—sink in. But then . . .

"Well, some years later, you find yourself talking to your child, who is of high intelligence, and saying: 'No, you cannot drive the car until you get a learner's permit.'

"And then, ten minutes later, you see your car being driven down the street by the same child you just told not to drive it." When the child gets back and gets out of the car, the following conversation ensues:

"Was that you driving the car?"

"Yes."

"Why?"

"Well, I just wanted to see if I could do it."

"But didn't I tell you not to drive it?"

"Yes."

"Well, if I told you not to drive the car, why were you driving it?"

"I don't know."

"Well, to me," Cosby went on, "that's brain damage. All children have that kind of brain damage. Parents should prepare themselves to face that fact."

As he raised his family, Cosby began to assume a few of

the traits of W. C. Fields, along with all the Mark Twain stuff he had grown up on.

Cosby was learning what it was all about. It was a hard life, and it wasn't all sugar and spice and everything nice. It was a lot of rats and snails, and puppy dog's tails.

In 1969, after *I Spy* wrapped up, Ennis was born— Cosby's first and only son. A reporter asked him the obvious question: how had Cosby ever decided to call his son "Ennis."

Cosby nonchalantly and somewhat deceptively said that he had simply made up the name, and pointed out that it meant:

"Trust nobody—and smile."

Some years later he told the same story with a slight variation. When he was asked if his son Ennis was named after the band leader Skinny Ennis, Cosby explained:

"My wife and I were just looking for odd names to give the children so they'd have an identification of their own instead of Tom Cosby, Roy Cosby, and so on, and we were just looking in the book one day and I said this is an odd name. On top of that, it has nothing to do with this kid because it means 'the ninth.' It's a Greek word. So I said, let it be that."

And it was that.

Six years after the birth of Ennis, the third Cosby daughter, Ensa, was born in the month of April. Then in 1977, the fifth child, Evin, arrived—another daughter. Four girls and one boy.

The Cosbys were now, since 1971, living in the big house in Amherst, where there was room to spare. Cosby couldn't help but think of the place in comparison to his own home in North Philadelphia in his youth. Sixteen rooms and 286 acres of ground for his family of seven, in contrast to two stories in a project for a family of four. There simply wasn't any valid comparison possible.

He remembered vividly how small the house had seemed

when the Cosbys had their big family reunions, with all the blood relatives congregating at the tiny house.

"When they had those big dinners—and by big I mean twenty people in this small, two-story house—the aunts would come and they would be so loud! And then the women would hit the men on the back and the kisses would go like that."

Cosby was six or seven at the time. He remembered how he had thought, "Oh, man! That's got to hurt!" He told how they were so happy to see one another, and how they hugged, and how the men would grab the women and swirl them around.

"That was okay, but those women looked like they would just tear—*tear*—the men up with the smackings on the back. And then, the laughter. And then, my grandfather with those stories down in the cellar. My mother reading to me.

"And when I was in the crib, I remember my brother James and I in the same crib, and my mother reading Mark Twain to us. And I was little then. And I had pajamas that you put your feet in. And they were all in one piece. And there was a flap—a flap in the back. You were locked in. Like in an LST. You know. Let Things Out. Close It Up."

(For the uninitiated, the LST [Landing Ship, Tanks] was an amphibious carrier of tanks used in combat during World War II; it was fully enclosed with armorplate when in motion across the water, but came unbuttoned to let forth the vehicles of war when it landed on a beachhead or promontory.)

Meanwhile, in the Amherst house, to the astonishment and relief of both Cosby and Camille, the children did display some evidence of growth and the achievement of a certain amount of maturity.

Of course, whatever growth was evident was due to the parental exertion of discipline on and the instilling of a sense of responsibility in the five children. A most difficult matter, Cosby pointed out once, this matter of discipline.

"It is the fact that we all have the same curse on us that goes all the way back to Genesis," he observed in the fashion of Mark Twain to a magazine editor. He went on to say that God told the children Adam and Eve, "I want you to look after the garden, but don't. . . ."

Cosby paused to explain. "That was where God made the first mistake, by saying to human beings, 'Don't.' And by using the other word, 'forbidden.'

"Because that was the first time Adam and Eve were really paying attention. And then they ate the fruit. Of all the things that are on the face of this earth that were available to them, these two brain-damaged people went directly to the thing that God said, 'Don't.' They committed the sin, and then blamed it on the snake.

"Anybody with children will see the parallel. The brain damage and the children doing exactly what you tell them not to do."

In Amherst, Cosby was working on the *Fat Albert* show, and one day he took his son Ennis down to watch him at work.

"Ennis was eight," Cosby recalled, "and had been watching the show for three years, but suddenly he looked at me with amazement and new respect."

"Dad," Ennis said to his father. "*You're* Fat Albert?"

Suddenly it was worth all the trouble it took to *be* Fat Albert!

In a *Saturday Evening Post* interview, Cosby tried to explain to Todd Klein how he kept ahead of his kids when they refused to do what he wanted them to do.

"I remember years ago when I was playing ball with my father in the backyard. I was a teenager then, and I found out I was quicker than he was.

"I was feeling all cocky." His father, however, wasn't having any nonsense from him. He just looked Cosby straight in the eye and observed coolly:

"You gotta sleep sometime."

Cosby always remembered that—and uses it to this day. Now:

"My own son is six feet four inches," he noted, "and I'm not far from letting him know that he can get as big as he wants to—but *he has to sleep sometime.*"

No matter how much Cosby talked to other people about his kids, he found himself always coming right back to proper discipline and punishment. Is it yes? Is it no? Is there a way to punish *right*?

In an *Essence* article, Cosby discussed the nitty-gritty of disciplining children.

"Whenever you decide to punish them, you must really and truly follow through on that punishment. . . . My wife Camille and I have just let them know point-blank that if this is some sort of battle, or some sort of war that has been declared, and they want to see how long we can stay in there with them—*we're not going anywhere.*"

At one time Cosby confessed that he had nurtured hidden dreams about family life—how he would love to be able to *come back* at a much later date and start out again with a family. But there was one special condition he'd insist on.

On *Nightwatch* he told Charles Rose:

"If I had to come back, I would enjoy coming back as a parent with wisdom. And I'd be only five years old, too. I'd start having my kids when I was five, so I'd have the same amount of energy that they have, because, you know, when they get that burst of speed around seven o'clock, and they're supposed to be tired and ready for bed, they get that kick, man. It's hard, when you're twenty-seven, twenty-eight, and you see a five-year-old put that burst in, and you see that energy flow, and the bodies giving, and they're trying to show you that they don't want to really go to sleep, and you're tired by that time, and you've worked all day.

"If I was five years old and had five kids, I'd be able to

keep up with them, put them all to bed. Yeah. I want to be that tall. I want to be about six one, but only five years old. And a father!"

Asked by a magazine editor if there were any special joys that he had gotten out of his family life, Cosby didn't need to think long before coming up with an answer.

Special joys? "None. Your children will be your children for the rest of your life. Now, that says it all. The only thing we want is for them to grow up and get out of the house. And we want them to do well."

Being away from home a lot as a professional entertainer caused Cosby to be an absentee parent during the more active portions of his career. Yet he never allowed it to affect the degree of control he exerted over his children.

He once told Phil Donahue that his situation was somewhat different from other men's. Although he did spend a great deal of time away from home when he was shooting on location, working the nightclub circuit, or whatever, when he came home, he was very much *there*.

"First of all, when I'm home, I'm *home*. I'm home twenty-four hours a day. I have lived with them. You have to trust me, I have lived with them. I know each one's behavior, their idiosyncrasies, and I know *them*. On top of that, Mrs. Cosby knows them very well. And Mrs. Cosby and I talk about the children."

On a lighter note, like most family men, Cosby still voices reservations about the need for and the success of Father's Day.

"Father's Day. That's a day we ought to get rid of. It's somewhere between Ground Hog Day and check-cashing Monday. We get presents that nobody else would accept, and we look at them, and we smile, and we thank people for them, and then they go away—but they know they've cheated on the presents.

"They know they had thirty dollars to spend, and they looked for something for two dollars and forty-five cents. People keep saying, 'I don't know what to get you,' but everything they buy, sooner or later your wife has to give away to the Salvation Army, or maybe you find the kids washing the car with it.

"The most memorable Father's Day present I ever got was a pair of booties—those fur things with rabbit ears and rabbit eyes. The last child gave them to me. I was very proud of them because they were warm and the ears flapped when I walked and the little black things rolled around in the eyes. I went downstairs and our dog is old and his sight is not good. He thought they were two rabbits attacking me, and he ate them while they were on my feet, and he thought he'd done a wonderful job."

But because of Father's Day, there's also Mother's Day, which, in the way of things, occurred first, *before* there was a Father's Day. Anyway. . . .

"My kids think Father's Day is a non-holiday, but Mother's Day is an important holiday. The reason is that mothers orchestrate the gifts they get, and know exactly what they want. Fathers don't."

Cosby has always hated to be assessed as a "perfect father." If ever asked why he is a "perfect father" and how he got that way, he usually answers the question by couching his words in this fashion:

"Ask me anything, I've got the answer.

"However, I should warn you that such answers tend to encompass a gamut of parental tactics from moving speeches on racial pride to outright bribery in the form of cold cash."

And then, of course, the inevitable question comes up wherever he goes.

"How do you rate yourself as a father, Mr. Cosby?"

"Well, I think I'm pretty good," he might say. "I think I'm pretty good. I think that the children know that I love them. I think that my children know that I am the kind of father who, no matter what happens, will still be pitching and still be giving to them to help them. They know that, whether they are sick or well, that I will be there. I think that's one of the things that's important in being a father."

Now that his family is growing up and maturing, Cosby finds even more aggravating questions like the one he was recently asked.

"Are you one of that special breed of the 'new and improved' father?"

Cosby minced no words to the interviewer:

"I don't think there is a 'new-and-improved-father' situation. You're fooling yourself if you think you've got new and improved males because you see three or four dudes out there doing diapers and dishes.

"That's like looking at Black America and saying, 'Isn't this wonderful?' because you can see a couple of black women and men in executive positions.

"I think you need to talk to some women out there who are divorced and single—and let them tell you about those males. To me, the 'new-and-improved' father just doesn't exist."

"Let's just suppose," the questioner goes on, "that you are all through raising your kids and that they have moved out of the house and aren't around anymore. Will there be an empty nest syndrome in your house? If there is, how will you cope with it?"

"There won't be any," Cosby says.

"Aren't you worried that all of a sudden you'll be standing there with Camille and the house will be empty and there'll be no sounds?"

Cosby's eyes light up. He grins.

"And we'll have sex. And *loud*. And nobody knocking on our door."

Erika. Erinne. Ensa. Ennis. Evin.

Cosby was asked not once but a hundred times: "How come all your kids have names that begin with an 'E'?"

"They begin with 'E' because 'E' stands for 'excellence,' " Cosby said.

Recently he was asked by a woman in the audience of a

Cosby with the Emmy he received in 1966 for his part on the hit series "I Spy." Cosby was the first black to win the award for a leading role in a television series. (AP/WIDE WORLD PHOTOS)

Cosby with Danny Thomas on a 1965 television special. (AP/WIDE
WORLD PHOTOS)

Arriving for the 1965 Academy Awards with his wife, Camille.

Cosby with "I Spy" co-star Robert Culp. (AP/WIDE WORLD PHOTOS)

Cosby at Desilu Studios where ''I Spy'' was produced.

On the ''Tonight Show'' with Johnny Carson in 1968.

With Mrs. Martin Luther King, Jr., and actor Sidney Poitier at the premiere of ''Uptown Saturday Night.'' (AP/WIDE WORLD PHOTOS)

Cosby also starred with Poitier in the movie ''Piece of the Action.''
(AP/WIDE WORLD PHOTOS)

Cosby and his television cartoon characters, including Fat Albert, in 1972. (AP/WIDE WORLD PHOTOS)

Cosby dribbles in for a shot in a charity exhibition game with the Harlem Globetrotters. (AP/WIDE WORLD PHOTOS)

Playing tennis with Australian Fred Stolle in a pro-am exhibition match in 1974. (AP/WIDE WORLD PHOTOS)

Cosby working out with the Howard University track team. (AP/WIDE
WORLD PHOTOS)

(Following page, top)
Posing for a poster celebrating National Library week. (AP/WIDE WORLD
PHOTOS)

(Following page, bottom)
With former President Jimmy Carter and cast members for a public
service television film. (AP/WIDE WORLD PHOTOS)

On the platform with Jesse Jackson at a fundraiser for Operation Push in Chicago. (AP/WIDE WORLD PHOTOS)

Sharing a laugh with fellow comedian Dick Gregory as he receives an honorary doctor's degree from Morehouse College in Atlanta in 1986. (AP/WIDE WORLD PHOTOS)

The cast of ''The Cosby Show.'' (AP/WIDE WORLD PHOTOS)

talk show if his interest in 'excellence' meant that he was a demanding person and a perfectionist at home.

He responded good-naturedly: "No. That was just my ego."

Erika, the oldest Cosby, was growing up, and she was questioned at length in a magazine article about life with her special father.

"Sometimes he'll take just one of us out to a movie and dinner so he can spend time with us individually," she told the interviewer. "It makes us all feel pretty special."

As for Ennis, he has turned out to be six feet four in height and very special to his father too.

The similarity between the families on NBC-TV's *The Cosby Show* and Cosby's real family in Amherst, Massachusetts, is striking of course: husband and wife, four daughters, and one son!

When the kids occasionally go down to the weekly taping of the show in Brooklyn, Ennis sometimes plays basketball with his fictional counterpart on the show, the character Theo played by Malcolm Jamal Warner.

It was no contest. Ennis's six-four towered over Malcolm's five-six!

CHAPTER FIVE

THE HUMAN CONDITION

WHEN BILL Cosby was very young he discovered
the human body. In many ways, it became the most
fascinating thing in his young life. As time went on, he
discovered that everybody else had a body, too; and to
them it was just as fascinating and interesting as it was to
him.

Later on, Cosby discovered that there was a generation
gap between all parents and all children; he discovered
that there was an even greater generation gap between
kids and their grandparents.

Soon he discovered age and what it did to you.

All these things became part of what he thought of as
the human condition. Here are some of his more tren-
chant thoughts on the human condition—physical, psychological, and spiritual.

In a piece he wrote for *Ebony* magazine, Cosby had
something to say about sleep.

"When I was twenty-five," he recalled, "I had to *force*
myself to go to sleep. Now I'm forty, and I *want* to go to
sleep. Sleep is a wonderful thing. I wish I had found out
about it earlier."

On the *Tonight Show* Cosby discussed exercise and the
fat lot of good it does to anyone who tries it.

"At my age, you're not building *character* anymore when you exercise. You're just trying to run off the fat that has collected because you can't get rid of it. And then, when you're running, your lungs come *outside*. They really do! They don't know *what* you're doing. They know you're forcing them, and they know there's no *reason* for this. So they come out and they look at you.

"And then they go back inside. And what I like about it is that all this stuff on you comes off, and you begin to take shape. But the shape is not like the one you had before. Because I never will get that one back. It's not gravity, exactly; it's just the fact that your muscles don't want to do it anymore.

"They know you sit a lot, that you watch TV, that even if they do jump, what are you going to do anyway? They know you have nothing in mind, and they just kind of slump down."

Cosby has enough comprehension of his bodily parts to know that they were and are always in conflict with one another, with the entire body ganging up on the leader inside the brain. Thus:

"By the time you reach middle age, you just take it for granted that you're going to always be able to straighten up. You've done it a million times. But suddenly, one day, the back decides to pay you back for all those things you did when you were fifteen and sixteen. The back says: 'Remember the time you said to lift the sofa and I told you I couldn't do it, and you made me do it anyway? Now take that!' And the back will bring you to your knees."

One of Bill Cosby's latest horrendous discoveries is the fact that his navel has apparently vanished from his body to seek out a life of its own somewhere far removed from him.

"My navel is all the way back *in* my body," he told Johnny Carson and Ed MacMahon one night on NBC-TV. "It's about here." He bent his arm around and pointed to the middle of his back. "I mean, it's all the way back *there*. My navel simply does not want to see light anymore.

"I don't think *this* ever happened to you. I got out of the shower. And this is embarrassing, but I'm going to tell it anyway. I got out of the shower—naked of course—and dried myself off. I'm facing the counter and I pick up my razor. Well, I drop the razor. I bend over to pick it up and . . . the water flows out of my navel . . . Water! I'm talking about *a cup of water!* A cup!"

Frequently all the various parts of Cosby's body are in mutiny against him. There's a kind of game these parts play, especially when you aren't looking. As Cosby told Brad Darrach of *Reader's Digest:*

"You eat a big dinner and tell yourself you'll get up at six o'clock the next morning and run it off. But when the alarm hits and the brain announces that it's time to get up, the legs say, '*I* didn't eat the food. If you want to run, have the *stomach* do it.' "

Cosby has recently realized that he is finally over the hill and that his memory banks are beginning to atrophy, if not disintegrate entirely.

"Another thing that goes—in addition to the body—at middle age is the memory. You find yourself walking into rooms and forgetting what you went in for, or standing around after a shower and trying to remember whether you've put on your deodorant or not, or getting into the car and driving off and then forgetting where you're going. And your family is no help because they keep moving things on you. Worst of all, although everybody forgets something sometimes, when you're older you *persecute* yourself for having forgotten."

Another pet hate that Cosby seems to have acquired in the past few crucial years is that of the accoutrements that go with his gym equipment and exercising machines. Most diabolical is the machine that tells you what your weight is.

"Weighing scales are usually accurate," Cosby admits ruefully, "but never *tactful*."

But after all, the aging process is simply a part of humankind's life that must be accepted, if not gracefully, at least realistically. Nevertheless, that doesn't mean that a person should be forced to *love* the idea of getting older and older—and older.

"There are, of course, some advantages that occur in middle age. But now that I'm forty and my mind has started to play tricks on me, I can't remember what they are."

In 1981 Cosby appeared in public—and on the *Tonight Show*—sporting a pair of glasses. Spectacles: prescription ground lenses in them, not shades for effect.

Probed by Carson, Cosby admitted that his eyes were growing older. *He* might not be, but his eyes were. After all, *he* couldn't be getting older. His grandfather lived to be ninety-eight years old.

Carson was curious. "Does aging *bother* you?"

"No," Cosby answered. "It doesn't bother me at all. I'm just happy to be here no matter what the punishment."

About the wearing of glasses to see better, he wrote at greater length.

"I knew something was wrong when I started having to make a face in order to see better. You see, your eyes wait until you're middle aged to pay you back for all that reading you did in the dark. Your eyes are also telling you that by the time you reach forty, if you haven't seen all the women you need to see, you can forget it.

"And the medical profession is at fault, too. You'd think that most of the people who use medicine are middle aged or older. Yet they still keep writing on prescription bottles in a size that only a twenty-year-old can read. You were standing there with the medicine bottle in your hand and you died because you couldn't read the directions!"

When Cosby was working on *The New Bill Cosby Show* in 1972 he adjusted his image to the more mod fashion. He took to wearing long sideburns and a mustache. George

Schlatter, his co-producer, killed the mustache. The brush simply *had* to go, he told Cosby. So did CBS. Cosby shaved down, but reluctantly:

"When you spend weeks growing a mustache you almost fall in love with it. I had a good, big, thick mustache once. Everything you drink with it, you drink twice."

And he made an interesting discovery in 1980, something akin to Archimedes' discovery of the law of displacement:

"When you reach middle age you find that everything you eat turns to gas!"

Well, the truth of the matter was that *everybody* was getting older. He wasn't alone. After all, it was just the way things were. And Cosby began noticing things.

"When wives and mothers turn forty, that's when they start to come in and make speeches.

" 'You know, I only have so many years left in my life.' It's funny to listen to. 'You know, I only have *so* much time in life *left*—'

"They start talking like Buck Jones and Tim McCoy. 'I'd rather go out on the prairie and bring the cattle in. I only have so much time. I'm not riding that same horse again. And you're going to have to pitch in here.' "

Again, there was that worry about his navel. A psychiatrist might have told him it had something to do with what his mother had told him when he was a youngster growing up in Philadelphia.

"My mother always used to warn me about playing with my navel. 'Pretty soon,' she said, 'air will come out and you'll fly around the room.' "

All in all, it's just part of the human condition, for which Cosby has his own philosophical comment to end all such other comments:

"What makes you think you're going to walk through this life having big fun?"

CHAPTER SIX

VIVE LA SIMILARITÉ

BILL COSBY came onto the national scene before the "black is beautiful" era of racial equality had changed the stance of the battle for civil rights from passive resistance to militant activism. Even so, his first jokes were ethnic; his streetwise characterizations were ethnic; his best lines and quips were race oriented.

"When I told racial jokes, the blacks looked at the whites, the whites at the blacks, and no one laughed until I brought them together, and then I had to tell the jokes all over again!"

Along with other comedians, Cosby could see that there was a no-win quality to the continued stereotype of racial jokes used in the battle for civil rights. What he tried to do was reach *all* the people, so, as he put it, folks would say:

"Hey, man, here's a black who *doesn't* use racial material!"

In so doing, Cosby came to feel that the best way to minimize the differences in the races was—in the words of the popular song—"to accentuate the positive and eliminate the negative."

Cosby's approach was similar to the master, Mark Twain who wrote about the universal man—the man who was the same as all his brothers. Adam, for example.

73

"I think the whole world's problem with dealing with black people, and people of color, and then on down the line—an Irishman versus an Italian—even if there are no black people, a Swede against a Swede, if there are no Irish or Italian people to turn around and look at. I think it's human beings, period, who cannot deal with each other.

"Back to what's written in the Bible: Adam and Eve, two sons. One kills the other! There's only *four* people. If that guy didn't like his brother, he could have gone to Hawaii.

"Frankly, there is hope for the future because God has a sense of humor, and we're funny to God. That's why we're still around."

In effect, Cosby's modus operandi was to make the attack positive by focusing on the *similarities* in people, not the *differences*.

Vive La Similarité!, as he might have put it, rather than *Vive La Difference*. Robert Culp, Cosby's co-star on *I Spy*, once summed it up in this way by showing how the relationship with Cosby was after they worked on the show:

"An absence of a statement was the idea. We did it with such success that finally people forgot he was black and I was white."

It did indeed turn out that way. Yet Culp saw one problem innate in the way Cosby was going at it.

"But he has got [himself into] a hell of a dilemma," he pointed out. "He's in danger of rejection because he isn't sharing [the blacks'] struggle, their pain, and their militancy."

It was an astute observation. Yet Cosby stuck to his guns, in spite of the malcontents.

Cosby was never one to tout what has been called "Black English." English to Cosby is English and always will be. This is the way he put it for an interview in *Essence* magazine.

"In this country, business is conducted in white English. That is a fact of life. You don't 'get down' when talking with the chairman of the board; you don't greet him with a big 'Hey!' and a brothers' handshake. You don't punctuate every sentence that makes sense with a 'right on'—not unless you want to be right out . . . on your ass.

"The black-is-beautiful era produced some fine values, but making up our own language is not one of them. That's lighting a fire that warms nobody. If we, blacks, are to succeed in business—and *we must*—then we must speak the language of industry. Ghetto-talk doesn't get anyone a job."

He believed strongly that the black person was in a continuing search for his real identity. It was, essentially, almost a life-or-death struggle.

"Our people were brought over here on a boat. Didn't ask nobody for a lift. Hell, we were having fun listening to the medicine men! But into the boat. People shoved together, babies dying. Nobody gave a damn. So how does the black know who he is, really?"

Bigotry always bugged Bill Cosby, because so many people were bigots without even *realizing* it. And he had things to say about Archie Bunker, the extremely long-lived and most successful bigot in the history of television:

"*All in the Family* would be over if Archie Bunker knew what his problem was. [It's bigotry, of course.] Names have a tendency to stay. Names like 'kike,' 'nigger,' and the rest of them never seem to die. Archie says them in his house where in his mind it's safe.

"I guess what I dislike most about him is that he never says what he does is wrong. Like a junkie shooting up, he's *enjoying* it."

Black associates with liberal pretensions were annoyed at Cosby when during the first of the civil rights demonstrations in the 1960s he refused to join the street marches. On his CBS-TV variety hour, broadcast in 1972, Cosby played in a skit with Harry Belafonte.

In it Belafonte pleaded with him to come and lend his

support in the battle for civil rights. Belafonte almost got down on his knees to Cosby.

"Come home, black brother!" he cried at the climax of the scene.

Cosby grimaced, frowned, and stared in disbelief. "To *Philadelphia*?"

Shades of W. C. Fields!

In a motion picture he made around that time there was a scene in which a sidekick was warning him about gambling, about how dangerous it was, and about the dire consequences that might possibly result—quoting Harry Truman's comment in 1952:

"If you can't stand the heat, stay out of the kitchen!"

Cosby: "I remember. I was in the kitchen when he said it."

By 1977 Bill Cosby had a pretty sharp and in-focus picture of the future of blacks and whites in America, and it was not particularly a happy one. But nevertheless, he elucidated it in an interview with an *Essence* writer.

"Let's just say that I'm pleased by some things that are happening. I'm pleased, for example, that an Andy Young has lit coals—coals people don't necessarily like to see burning. But let's not forget that only laws are suppressing the undercurrent of racism that still exists in America today.

"Recently when I saw *The Deep* with a white audience, they were screaming: 'Kill the nigger!'

"But uptown, blacks viewing the same flick were yelling just as loud: 'Stick it to the white bastard!'"

In a *Scholastic Senior* article Cosby explained one reason why he had chosen to be an entertainer and a comedian.

"You know, it's all because I want to be accepted. That's why I tell jokes. I discovered that people would laugh at my jokes—and that meant they *liked* me, they accepted me. It was even better when they started throwing *money!*"

And what about the struggle against racism? Could racism be eradicated? If not, was there any answer to it? How did you handle it?

"The answer to racism is to know how to deal with it. When I was in high school, I was already playing semi-pro baseball with a bunch of black dudes. Yet, when I tried out for the varsity team, the coach says, '*Boy*, you don't know how to throw a ball.'

"So I walked off that field and onto the one where they were holding track tryouts.

"In other words, racism has always been alive, well, and living in America. But the real issue has always been: How are you going to let it or *not* let it affect you? I chose not to let it get to me by learning to do business."

For a piece in *Look* magazine, as early as 1967 at the height of the civil rights movement, Cosby responded to being badgered by reporters and writers about his reluctance to join his black brothers—Sammy Davis, Jr., Dick Gregory, etc.—to travel through white neighborhoods and experience the slings and arrows of outrageous white wrath.

"Why don't you go out with them?" he was asked.

"Fear, man," answered Cosby. "Fear."

They even asked him what he thought about passive resistance and its effectiveness in bringing about equal civil rights for blacks.

"In no way should I take a blow from a man because he's white and because I want to show him my love," Cosby responded.

At another time he tempered that statement somewhat. "My glands don't secrete that way. I just can't see praying for someone who's kicking you, and I don't want to go where there's tear gas unless I have some tear gas to throw back at the guys who're throwing it at me."

The trouble, Cosby felt, wasn't all on one side. That is, it wasn't all on the side of the so-called "right-wingers."

Even some of the "liberals" weren't so lily-white and so liberal when you came right down to it.

"Blacks have been in the United States for five hundred years," he pointed out. "But I get into a cab in New York and some guy who just came over on the boat, *he* doesn't want to pick me up because he's an American—dig? If Europe is so liberal, the way we hear tell, how come the moment this guy arrives here he's an instant bigot?"

And the kids? What about the kids in the civil rights movement?

"Kids ask the best questions," he said once. "One asked me what were my goals for the black people."

Cosby paused. "There's just one word," he said. "Equality. Period."

Cosby told others that he meant it when he said he'd be teaching junior high in a few years—"in an underdeveloped neighborhood."

In 1965 it was probably the most exciting thing in the world to be the first black star of a dramatic network television program, a show that was a smash hit as well as a breakthrough for black performers.

The co-star of *I Spy* once said:

"Because I was first, the network and the advertisers were nervous about how I should act, on camera *and off* . . .

"There were a dozen thin lines I was supposed to walk. I had to dress and talk like 'them,' or I was considered uneducated. But if I dressed or spoke too well, as in *better than*, then I was threatening—and that was no good.

"With all this, I still had to live with me in that role, making the character acceptable not just to white America but to me and to blacks everywhere."

Cosby had little sympathy for white people who put on blackface to amuse each other, like the stars of the famous *Amos 'n' Andy* show:

"If they want to look funny, let them put on blue or green faces."

A white woman reporter from the *New York Times* asked Cosby whether or not he felt "accepted" by white people. Cosby answered the question by posing another instead:

"You married? Okay, then. Say I work with your husband and one day he says to me, 'Hey, man, will you go pick up my wife for me? I got something to do.'

"So I pick you up, and I have to put a sign on the car saying:

THIS WOMAN IS NOT MY GIRLFRIEND. SHE IS MARRIED TO
SOMEBODY ELSE WHO IS ALSO WHITE.

"When you belong to a minority group . . . you have to walk so that you don't upset the people who are in a position to give you the next step so you can eventually walk by yourself."

Cosby put it into focus once and for all about being a black comedian as opposed to a nonethnic comedian:

"Suppose, as a kid, I wanted to grow up and be like Charlie Chaplin. That doesn't mean I want to grow up to be white. It means I want to be funny, to bump into a pole, to fall in love with a beautiful woman and be very clumsy about giving her a rose. But people want to force us into saying,

" 'Here is my blackness.'

"Well, I don't think anybody really learns anything from that."

In spite of the fact that he grew up with the image in mind of an "artist" as a person uninvolved with the sordidness of money, Cosby recently discussed his ability to handle money and its importance to him.

"My manager took care of all the business while I handled the performing. My checks were signed for me. *They* had power of attorney. Often, I had no idea how much I was earning or how much was being spent. Not that they wouldn't tell me, I just didn't ask. I figured,

'I'm an artist and an artist shouldn't be bothered by business.' Which is a cop-out and *bullshit!*

"Today I make as much money as I ever did—about seven figures per year—and I handle every penny of it. I've learned how. And what I couldn't learn, I got from others whom I hired and who report to *me*. I made myself learn about business.

"Today only Camille or I sign the Cosby checks. I found a conservative accounting firm. I told them: 'No messing around. Pay it in full and pay it clean.' I didn't want to get hit in the back of the head later with a back-taxes bill that causes professional and personal suicide. In short, I assumed responsibility for my life."

All in all, though, Cosby's impression of the black in society today is far different from what he felt it to be only a few years back.

"The black's whole image is changing. He's no longer being thought of as shiftless, lazy; now he's thought of as a tough son of a bitch."

CHAPTER SEVEN

THE SPORTING LIFE

FROM THE beginning, Bill Cosby was always interested in sports; from the early years on the street, through school, through his navy service, through college later on, and even after he had become a star.

Sports is part of the entertainment world, and as such lends itself triumphantly to the humorous touches of anyone like Bill Cosby.

Here are some of Cosby's best remarks, including some reminiscences of his early days that are side splitting mostly because they occurred without preparation.

His accolade to one of his early role models is appropriate in this spot:

"I had an idol—Jackie Robinson. He made it happen for blacks in baseball by using his talents, never his rage, to express his blackness. I felt that if in my ball park I did my job as well as Robinson did his, I would also therefore be moving us down the road a piece."

During his years at Temple University, Cosby served as anchor man on the varsity relay track team. He won some records and didn't win some others. On one memorable afternoon, however, it became a Cosby afternoon in spectacular fashion.

Picture 70,000 track fans in Philadelphia's Franklin

81

Field, watching him and his teammates putting out their best effort. And picture also what *really* happened, in Cosby's own words as he told it to *True* magazine:

"We're all lined up there, with itchy feet, waiting to get the baton and take off. But as my man gets near the passing point, the baton hits his leg and flies up in the air.

"What does this cat do? He just starts to laugh! All the other anchor men are off and running, and me? I'm standing there waiting for this nut to stop laughing, pick up the baton, and give it to me.

"Finally, he retrieves it and walks over to me with the damned thing. *Walks!*

"I took it and bopped him right on the head with it, which is when the fans began screaming with laughter.

"But that's not the end of it. Old Cosby's a team player to the end. I took off after those runners like a madman. I'm running and running, and passing one guy, and then passing another, and then I get what you call in the sports business if you're a runner 'rigor mortis.' It's a freeze-up from the effort of running.

"First my muscles freeze, then my chest, then my legs. I fall down, a beaten man if ever there was one, and while I'm down, the cat I had hit over the head comes up, takes the baton, and bops me back with it. I couldn't dream up a routine *that* funny!"

Between takes on his current Number One show Cosby and members of the cast were talking to some college girls who play basketball at New York University.

Cosby winked and had this to say to the black girl who played guard:

"Now don't you go passing between your legs and dribbling behind your back just to impress the white folks!"

High school sports for Cosby weren't quite what they became when he got to college and later joined the navy. He was, at that time, pretty much an also-ran.

"I was on the ninth football team, which was made up

of me and ten other guys from the remedial gym class. All we had to do was look at the parallel bars and they gave us a *D*. I never got into the game and I had to give my jersey to the guy who had his ripped."

One year he wrote a book about tennis—sort of tongue-in-cheek Cosby-type tennis, if you will. One of his famous lines from the book reads:

"If you and the ball happen to arrive at the same place at the same time, don't panic; body spasms will not help you execute the stroke."

When he was just starting out in the nightclub circuit, Cosby turned his hand to writing pieces for the paper to publicize himself. One of them appeared in the *Chicago Daily News*, and contained the following climax of a piece that had to do with playing football in the streets of Philadelphia.

" 'Charlie!' I'd say. 'You go down ten steps, cut left behind the black Chevy, count to ten, then jump up on the hood. Bobby, you run in Brown's house and wait in the living room. Ronnie, here's ten cents; go down to Third Street, catch the J bus, and have the driver open the door at Eighth street. I'll fake it to you. The rest of you guys go long.'

"The play would start, and somebody'd always yell, 'Over here! Over here!'

"That was a signal. I'd throw the ball without looking, and it would almost hit my mother. Because all the mothers in the neighborhood knew that call 'Over here!' and my mom would use it to stop the game and make me come home to do my rotton old homework."

At a party a friend once seriously asked Cosby why he didn't become an athlete rather than a comedian. "You've got the body, man, you've got the guts!"

Cosby looked astonished. "I would have *killed* myself on the football field to make a lousy fourteen thousand dollars a year!" he snorted.

Later on, at the same gathering, someone who had

heard him talk about football brought up the subject again, accusing him not of being a comedian, which seemed all right, but of being—gulp!—a television *commercial* actor!

Cosby came up with this reasoning:

"Had I not gone into show business, I would have played football for the New York Giants. I would have tackled Jim Brown. And he would have broken my back. And I would have been paralyzed from here down, because I love football. I could have been paralyzed trying to tackle Jim Taylor, too. That's why I'm doing E. F. Hutton."

One magazine reported that the popularity of karate had always puzzled him—does, for that matter, to this very day!

"There must be twenty-three million karate schools in New York alone. I imagine that this is because, after you've been graduated from a karate school, there is no better feeling than knowing you can wipe out your whole neighborhood!"

Things changed for Bill Cosby when he became a famous television star. But he continued his interest in sports as recreation. Nevertheless, the sports scene in Beverly Hills and Bel Air was somewhat different from the streets of Philly.

He wrote about it in a *Look* magazine piece.

"When I used to play basketball in the playgrounds you didn't go to a stranger and introduce yourself. You had to prove yourself first. No names.

And the dialogue would go something like this:

"Over here, my man."

"Yeah, nice play, my man."

"Later on," Cosby wrote, "if you *earned* it, you'd be *given* a name: Gunner, My Man, or Herman. Or Shorty, or something.

"Now when we play Celebrity Basketball in Hollywood, they come out on the court and it goes like this."

Very *polite*: "Hi. My name is Such and Such. I'm from So Forth and So On."

Cosby: "Oh! How nice to meet you."

"But later on," Cosby went on, "during the game, I forget the cat's name anyway, and I just go right back to the usual."

And so it was: "Over here, my man. I'm here in the corner, my man."

Cosby: "And I'm back in the old neighborhood!"

Like all Americans, Cosby has a dream, too. In his dream there are many overtones. Listen:

"There are five of my people playing for the Boston Celtics, and the Irish people love it. Someday there's going to be a team called Black Power, and there'll be five white guys dribbling up the court.

"I hope I live to see it. Some of this gunk has got to clear up."

CHAPTER EIGHT

THE EDUCATOR/ENTERTAINER

WHEN BILL Cosby dropped out of Temple University to pursue a career on the entertainment circuit, his mother, according to Ponchitta Pierce in a *Readers Digest* article, took to her bed in shock and spent seven weeks there before she was able to get up again.

Education meant that much to her—and her son's defection from it was a terrible disappointment.

In the long run, Cosby's instincts proved to be right: he *did* indeed make a success—and an astonishing one at that—out of his talent in the rather precarious field of entertainment.

But by that time he had already dropped out of school *twice*—once from high school to join the navy and again from college to become a comic. A psychological pattern was being established. And yet, in his mind, Cosby had never really forgotten about his lapsed education, even during the halcyon days of his initial success.

Secretly, he was *determined* to go back to school and finish up with a degree—perhaps even *more* than a degree.

And, of course, he did.

But it too him six years to get that degree, and, along with it, a master's degree, *and* a doctorate in education.

It all really began to come together in 1971, with the

inception of *The Electric Company* show, broadcast over PBS. This Bill Cosby show was dedicated to improving the reading skills of children on the grammar-school level. It was a somewhat simplistic method of teaching, but Cosby fitted right in, trying to show the children who watched how to tell a "d" from an "e," and making jokes and songs up about letters and words and about reading.

Cosby never made much money out of the show, but it was a breakthrough of sorts for him; it showed that he was potentially a successful educator as well as a successful entertainer. The two do not usually go together gracefully.

No one drew much salary from the show—nothing on Public Broadcasting did at that time—and most of the staff did it for the experience and for the fun of it.

There was even a research team that worked out the techniques of teaching on the small television screen—a new consideration at the time. It took time and money to find out what worked and what did not work.

During the first year—1971—Cosby found himself working sometimes eighteen hours a day. This was difficult, because his family was back in Amherst, and he was on the set doing his job late.

How many times he must have thought to himself: "The hell with this, I'm splitting for home; no way am I doing this stuff for this money from seven in the morning till ten at night!"

Yet he did stick it out. And the show was a really exciting *new* thing, along the lines of *Sesame Street.*

Some of the best sketches were the ad libs that the group did, and these extemporaneous sessions helped Cosby hone his talents, which had always been strong in off-the-wall material.

Nevertheless PBS was PBS, and in a way, the audience was somewhat limited. Cosby was thinking about the big-time, about Saturday morning network stuff, where he could *really* teach lots of kids.

And so the concept of his second educational show, *Fat Albert and The Cosby Kids*, was born. Unlike *The Electric Show*, it was going to be a cartoon series, with Cosby doing the voice-overs, and also appearing as Bill Cosby to introduce the show each week.

Later on in *The New Fat Albert Show*, he would come on with this injunction to all the children watching:

"Here's Bill Cosby coming at you with music and fun, and if you're not careful, you may learn something."

That was the key. That *was* the message. Cosby conceived the show as more than simple entertainment for a Saturday morning. There was a serious educational purpose in mind. Cosby wanted not only to teach kids to read and write but he wanted to provide them with behavior models and sociological values—only of course he never intended to use those terms to them.

"The way I see the show," Cosby said, "it will be so casual in its teaching, the children will never know they're being taught. It will have Fat Albert and Old Weird Harold and those other characters I made up, but they will get themselves involved in things like mathematical equations and what geometry is all about and why."

Cosby knew where to go to get talent to make this educational stuff work. He appointed a group of educators as advisors. Gordon L. Berry, an assistant dean at UCLA was made head of the panel.

"When I selected the panel of advisers," Berry said, "I contacted prestigious people in the field of anthropology, psychiatry, sociology, child development, communication theory, and so forth.

"All of the team assembled are very busy. If they aren't giving their time for consultation on this project, they'd be doing several other things. So I naturally made it very clear that we would not merely provide a rubber stamp of approval for the network."

Careful attention was paid to the scripts and the endings, the concepts, and the ideas that involved proper child development.

"For instance," Berry pointed out, "a script about a prankster was called to our attention. We agreed a program should be done about a prankster, but they should not show the kind of prank that traumatized a child or one that was hostile, such as the flower that squirts water. And in the case of the kid that's the prankster, there should be negative feedback."

The great amount of attention that was paid to the conception of the story lines and to the writing of the show gave it excellent educational content. In its lifetime— it played from September 1972 to 1979 when it became *The New Fat Albert Show*—it won any number of awards. It also won that which made Cosby's heart glow: high audience ratings.

Over six million kids fell in love with Bill Cosby. He had said it himself many times:

"I can be silly. I can be grown-up. I can be an older brother. I can be just a funny man that they know."

But Bill Cosby was much more than just a funny man they knew. He had a tremendous rapport with children of all kinds. Cosby always understood children around him—even when he was grown up—because he had been a Renaissance "kid" himself. That is, he was the ultimate child in his appreciation of and puzzlement at life. Most of the fun in listening to Cosby communicating with children is a realization that Cosby still has that innocence, that wide-eyed amazement that sense of wonderment at what is going on around him. It makes him just one big grown-up kid himself!

But more than simple understanding is involved in Cosby's success in the educational field. He understands the bridge that links children and adults. It is partly due to his instinctive warmth and "heart."

"Most parents' mistake is taking kids for granted," he said once. "All we have to do is give them bread to go to the flicks and buy records. But man, if you don't let them feel that heartbeat, there's just no love."

And he gave them love, even on that tiny screen. It was partly his persistent innocence, even in maturity.

"As a child," he told a reporter recently, "I always wondered about where 'kingdom come' might be, since my mother had threatened so many times to kick me there—along with my brothers.

"Worse than that, I wondered what I'd have to do if my mother kicked Russell there and then told *me* to go out and bring him back!"

That's fantasy land, strictly Cosby-type.

Or here he is as a kid, standing on the Philadelphia street in all his innocence and wonder, staring at a street excavation and saying in bemused astonishment:

"Hey, did you know that was *dirt* down there under the cement in the sidewalk? I thought the cement kept right on going down and down!"

Or the simplicity of this statement that gets to the essence of secondary education: "Everything I ever made in metal shop turned out to be an ashtray!"

Or the observation of the way he handles himself with a youngster not at all favorably disposed to him and insolent enough to ask him, almost with a sneer, "How come you're so famous?"

"Well," Cosby said to the freckle-faced youngster slowly, "one day I was just standing on the street with hundreds of people walking by, and they just took a vote, and I became famous!"

Whatever it was—Cosby's charisma as a star, his ability to communicate with children, or the superior concept of the show—*Fat Albert and The Cosby Kids* was a big hit with the public and with the critics.

In 1973 it won the Children's Theater Association Seal of Excellence.

All this dabbling at the borders of education began to pay off in another way for Bill Cosby. His dream of making it up to his mother for dropping out of school *twice* was suddenly in the works again.

Dr. Dwight Allen at the University of Massachusetts was approached and decided to make the *Fat Albert* show a part of a projected master's degree program for Cosby. In other words, working on the *Fat Albert* show, he would be earning college credit by turning in scripts just as if they were term papers.

He would also be working with professors and educators in evaluating the techniques being used in the combination of education and entertainment.

Once the thesis was approved, Cosby was on his way. Its title was typical of theses titles: "An Integration of the Visual Media Via *Fat Albert and The Cosby Kids* into the Elementary School Curriculum as a Teaching Aid and Vehicle to Achieve Increased Learning."

Cosby even wrote workbooks and teaching guides to help adapt the *Fat Albert* shows to classroom use.

"If I can keep even one confused, unhappy kid from going down the drain, from dropping out of school," Cosby vowed, "I'll have made a real contribution."

On a May afternoon in 1976, it all came together on the campus of the University of Massachusetts in Amherst, not far from the Cosby home.

As Cosby said later, "If Mom were dead, she would have gotten up to come. She always told me education is a must. Her tears made it all worthwhile."

But Anna was living on the Cosby farm, and was there to see the dream of her life come true.

And, later on, "You know, on the day of graduation, the ceremony pumped up all kinds of inner feelings," Cosby confessed. "It was a very emotional thing. While I was working on the doctorate, I wasn't aware of its import, of what it meant to me. I was too wrapped up in the work. I loved the research and the writing of my dissertation. I truly had a love affair with the learning.

"But it all passed without my feeling much of anything until graduation, until the speeches. Then I suddenly felt, 'This is it! *I've* done it!' I got all choked up. I think I would have cried if someone just at that moment hadn't tapped me on the shoulder and asked: 'May I have your autograph?' That snapped me back to reality."

The educator *and* entertainer: not a bad image for Bill Cosby. Like Mark Twain, his mentor, he was able to provide humor *and* little tidbits of knowledge at the same time.

Now Cosby could look back on one of his favorite lines and know that it did not any longer pertain to him:

"I played my whole youth," he once had said, "and every day I'm sorry for it."

With the concepts of education in mind, Cosby would deal with problems that had to do with children and with the raising of children.

"Most parents' mistake is taking kids for granted," he had said. "All we have to do is give them bread to go to the flicks and buy records. But man, if you don't let them feel that heartbeat, there's just no love."

And he is able to give his philosophical and personal ideas more clout with what he has learned about educational methods.

"I tell my kids that I'm going to leave them an awful lot of money," he told Alex Haley, "but that nobody is getting anything unless they have a formal education and can understand what to do with that money."

To reinforce what he is saying, he quotes what Sophie Tucker said a long time ago:

"I've been poor and I've been rich, and rich is better."

And he can fend off interviewers who are trying to prove something-or-other. For example, to one who asked him recently if he could be a full-time "Mr. Mom," Cosby responded,

"I was born in 1937, and at that time society was teaching me that I was the breadwinner, that I was the person to hold down two jobs in order to support a $35,000 home, and maybe two cars. I mean, that's what I was brought up to do, along with thinking that my wife would have children, and we would raise a family. No tea for two, you know—soup for seven!"

"Do you think you missed something," the interviewer went right on, "marching off to work all those days and leaving Camille and the kids at home?" The idea apparently was to make him feel like an antifeminist.

"Well, if I hadn't, I would have missed a pay check."

The educator/entertainer had also learned how to handle more difficult questions that came up regarding feminism.

"Having a child is somewhat different today from having a child say, a hundred years ago," an interviewer said. "Women now have a choice to have a child or not to have a child. Do you believe that a woman should have such a choice?"

Cosby pondered a moment. "I met a woman with seven children. She was thirty-six years old." When Cosby asked her why she had seven children, she replied:

"Because I keep falling asleep."

Cosby frowned. "I don't know if there's *really* a choice or not."

In September 1983 Cosby received the *Harvard Lampoon* humor magazine's first "Elmer Green" award for lifetime achievement in comedy. Green is the longtime curator of the humor magazine.

Cosby wound up the proceedings by enjoining his guests: "This joint costs fourteen thousand dollars a year, so let's get back to your rooms and hit the books!"

The educator/entertainer is not afraid to give advice to anyone who asks. Here's the advice he gave to a man on how to keep his marriage relationship fresh even when there was a new baby in the house—a time that is very rocky in any couple's life. Particularly so for the man, who is somehow at odds and ends—the extra guy at the party, so to speak.

Here's how Cosby advised him to keep things straight:

"Well," Cosby noted, "first of all, your wife is the older one. That's how you can tell who *that* one is. And she's generally taller than the others. Now, you'll know who you are. You're the husband. The biggest one in the house—the biggest baby."

Then, asked if he would like to be a grandfather, Cosby put on his educator's glasses and said:

"I would like it, yes. But I'm afraid, because my grandfather never could remember our names. He had thirteen grandchildren, and yet he called everybody Stephen. We didn't mind, because he'd say 'Oh, Stephen,' and we'd say, 'Hi, Grandad,' and then he'd give you fifty cents. And the man died broke, because the other kids in the neighborhood found out he didn't know, and they all lined up and they just let him call them Stephen, and the man died broke."

In many ways, of course, Cosby has been a grandfather before—at least, in a professional sense. How come?

"When I do a routine I am usually playing three fathers all the time—my grandfather, my father, and myself," Cosby notes. "I mean, there are certain things that I love about the way my father reacted to me, and they're funny, and I play him sometimes. And then the other times I play by grandfather. And then 70 percent of the time I play myself. It's a role that I know very, very well."

Asked about homework and maturity in the scheme of things, Cosby ventured:

"All the money in the world will not buy you a kid who will do homework, or maturity for a kid who needs it. It may buy a kid who knows how to *buy*."

The educator/entertainer has words of advice to a pregnant woman about to have a child:

"You'll find out how brilliant God is," he says. "God made a baby this size, and it's a thing that makes a lot of noise sometimes. As you get used to it, then it starts to *really* do things, and then you begin to question yourself, your judgment, and you'll never really be sure of yourself—or the kid. You'll be happy and you'll know love, and you'll know giving. You'll know an awful lot of things. And you'll become confused sometimes, for example, over what's more improtant—your child, or your husband."

In April 1986 Cosby received an honorary degree in fine arts from the University of Massachusetts, in no small way because of the tremendous popularity and critical success of *The Cosby Show*.

"All I do," the premier American educator/entertainer commented during the ceremony, "has to do with some form of education, some form of giving a message to people."

CHAPTER NINE

THE COSBY SHOW

AFTER BILL Cosby's disastrous television venture in 1976, he did not try anything new for quite a long time. He had made his fortune, and some people thought he might be relaxing and enjoying life.

He *was* enjoying life, but he was thinking about a new show. As he put it:

"I got tired of seeing television shows that consist of a car crash, a gunman, and a hooker talking to a black pimp. It was cheaper to do a new series than to throw out my family's television sets."

What Cosby knew and what the television pundits and experts did not know was that the type of audience reaction typical of the late 1970s was no longer necessarily *automatic*. It was, in fact, a time for change.

Whenever Cosby brought a new idea to the attention of either a motion picture or television mogul, it was generally cast out for one reason or another. What these people really wanted, Cosby thought, was the kind of "blaxploitation" he loathed. "Blaxploitation" is a Cosbyism for "black-exploitation," what Lewis Carroll used to call a portmanteau word.

During an interview, Cosby once imitated the way he

saw movie and television moguls talking about show business:

"Give them some sex, some guns, and some cocaine to capture the black audience. It is a proven formula, man! Maybe they will throw you a *Sounder,* but in the end it is easier to throw some dude five hundred thousand dollars and tell him to give with the sex, tits, and coke."

And that was *not* what Cosby believed in. What he believed in was a show about a family, much like his own, faced with problems, much like his own problems, and dealing with them in a fashion that would amuse, enlighten, and teach people who tuned in.

And so: *The Cosby Show,* on NBC-TV, starting in 1984. The following quotes and anecdotes are all related to the conception and making of the show.

During the making of one scene between Cosby and his television wife, Clair, played by Phylicia Ayers-Allen Rashad, the script called for him to come into the bedroom where she is still sleeping. He is carrying a breakfast tray with a croissant and butter and jelly on it.

He gets into bed and begins eating it. She wakes up and asks him to share it with her. He breaks off a tiny piece, puts butter and jelly on it and hands it to her. She makes a face and sticks it on his forehead. They both laugh.

Then she gives him a kiss, running her hand down the side of his arm to try to grab the croissant away from him.

The scene played right up to that point, with Phylicia giving Cosby a peck, and then fumbling as she tried to find the croissant. The director yelled to stop the tape.

"You can't do it that way!" he told her. "You *really* have to kiss this man."

Phylicia protested. "I can't kiss the man and find the thing at the same time!"

There was dead silence. Cosby immediately jumped up and said: "Quick! Somebody call my wife and tell her there are no problems because this woman can't kiss and find the thing at the same time!"

Not infrequently Bill Cosby's penchant for clowning around and ad-libbing remarks and gestures breaks up the cast and causes a shambles when the taping of the show is running late against a deadline.

At a recent production at the NBC-Brooklyn studios, Cosby finally called a halt to the proceedings and stepped out in front of the stage, right in the spotlight. He stared sternly at the mixed audience out there and asked them to put an end to the laughter and the applause.

"I'm doing it all wrong, and you're just encouraging me!"

Recently a member of the cast was married during the filming season with a great deal of media interest. It was through Cosby that Phylicia Ayers-Allen met Ahmad Rashad, the ex-football player. They became engaged, and then were married. Cosby acted as "father" to Phylicia and "gave her away" to the groom.

Later Cosby told Phylicia's mother that he was sure the marriage would work out.

"When *I* give 'em away, they *stay* given away!"

Not only is Cosby a workaholic, but he is also a perfectionist, members of his show troupe say. Cosby doesn't really think so. Certainly he wants the best for the show when he is dealing with material from outside.

"They say I'm a perfectionist. I'm not. Once again, it's all in the eye of the beholder. All I've asked anybody to do is not come back and give me some material that could have been done at eight o'clock when they say they stayed up till four in the morning to do it.

"They didn't do their best the first time. There's an awful lot of child in all of us. I mean, people especially in the entertainment business, those who work around the production staff. You say to somebody, do so forth and so on, and the person comes back and says, 'Well, you know—'

" 'Look. Did you look over this?'

"They say, 'Well—'

"And the person goes to someone else, and says, 'Gee, what does he want me to do anyway?'

"I was once reading a finished script and took out thirty-two pages. And the guy who wrote it says, 'Gee whiz! He treats the script like an outline.'

"Well, of course I did! Because it wasn't right. I'm not punishing anybody, but I don't think I would be fair to the public and the people viewing the show if I let what I didn't like go out.

"And when it was brought back, it was better. But the *grumblings* that went on, and, Whoa!, we don't want to do this! And some of the people left because I did make changes.

"But I remember writing a script myself. I thought it was the most brilliant thing I'd ever seen. After we sat down at the table and read it through, I tore out all of it. Everything except the introduction. So that was my work. That was my soul. My heart. And I tore it out. But, you see, it was wrong."

The youngest member of the cast is Keshia Knight Pulliam, who plays Rudy on the show. Here's how Cosby feels about her.

"When Keshia first started, of course we had a problem with her. She's a baby, and dealing with a baby and her embarrassment, or at a certain time having to work and not really caring about millions of dollars, she might decide that she just doesn't want to be there at that time. But now she's a grown woman of seven, and quite professional, and will even have nerve enough to tell me that what I said wasn't in the script, and she has *no* idea of what I'm saying."

With Harry F. Waters, a *Newsweek* writer, Cosby was discussing a possible trip to South Africa to photograph a few segments on location. As he was spinning it out in his usual fashion off the top of his head, he thought of a couple possible script ideas:

"I'll probably show Cliff as just another American tourist being unable to learn a foreign language. Of course, we may use a great *black* hunter to take him around!"

Matt Robinson, a writer on the show, was reminiscing once about the "good old days," pointing out that he and Bill Cosby both had summer jobs together as lifeguards at the municipal swimming pools in Philadelphia, even though Cosby went to Temple and Robinson to Penn State.

"The kids at my pool take the soap home," Robinson was complaining to Cosby.

"The kids at *my* pool bring their laundry!" Cosby shot right back.

At another time, Robinson came in with an idea about the excesses of teenage boys in pleasing their girlfriends. And that inspired a Cosby reminiscence:

"There was a kid in my neighborhood who had his girl's name, Barbara, tattooed across his chest—and *misspelled* it!"

Actor Malcolm-Jamal Warner plays Theodore, Cliff Huxtable's son on the show. He recalled one incidence of Bill Cosby's automatic humor:

"I remember one day Keshia [Rudy on the show], who is only seven, was supposed to run and jump on the stage for a scene. She was scared, and when she finally did it, she fell backward, hit her head, and started crying. Her mother ran over and tried to calm her down. But Mr. C. made Keshia start laughing by falling on the floor and kicking and screaming and wailing like he was hurt, too."

Cosby is many things to the people in the cast. To Phylicia Ayers-Allen Rashad, he has what she calls the "most unusual and spontaneous sense of humor" she has ever seen.

"An example: We're on the set one day, going through the rehearsal with the cameras. There's a plant over in the corner, a big, tall plant. He walks over to the plant and grabs it, making believe it is eating him. The cameramen were stretched out on the floor laughing and we were immobilized for fifteen minutes. He always comes up with spontaneous stuff like that."

To a young man who is also an aspiring comedian, Cosby took time out of his busy day on the set to explain his views of comedy and how to achieve it:

"Observe people closely, and use situations around you with which you are familiar. There always should be some basis in fact in our kind of humor."

Bill Cosby conceived *The Cosby Show,* and everything that is in it springs from his conception of it. These are a number of his thoughts about the show.

"I hope I have enough time to say what I really want to say [in it]. To talk about all those little moments we spend as parents to work out things; to be able to deal with a happiness and a love; to be able to draw laughs, without really crunching each other, or putting a hatred in; to really show kids at times, as they are, how they can get under your skin, and how you can come back again; to show that husband and wife can romance, without being so blatant about knowing that the next moment they're going to have sex; that a man's macho is not in turning one leg over and getting on top of the woman; that, in fact, it's the way a husband and wife can smile at each other, or a touch, or to do something with a flower, with a cup, you know, just a look; because couples become sort of in tandem to touch, to feel, to look, to think about."

And maybe Bill Cosby did that, because he confessed recently that this one meant more than any of his others. Because:

"I hardly ever watch my work, but with this show it's different. I watch every week. And at the end of every segment I find myself with a smile on my face because I really *like* that family and the feeling they give me.

"Last night I looked around at the people who were watching with me. They too were smiling, and they didn't even seem aware of my presence. Dr. Cliff Huxtable, up there on the screen, was an entirely different person to them—as he was to me. If I can so separate myself from a character I'm playing and enjoy him, I must be doing something right."

His old buddy Bill Culp would have agreed with that assessment. He had already made his own personal comment about the show and its star:

"The character he's playing is very close to the real Bill Cosby. He's taken off all the veils."

CHAPTER TEN

COSBYANA

THERE ARE pieces of Bill Cosby that do not fit into any special category, but are so typically Cosby especially since they were delivered when he was simply being himself and not performing written material.

Here are a number of Cosby's sayings or remarks exchanged with journalists and interviewers that are so much the man that they stand on their own as exactly how he—and only he—could say them:

Although he was examined and found to be "gifted" in an intellectual sense, Cosby did not take gracefully to education during his formative years. He recalled one test he had labored over.

"On some exam they gave me nine problems, and I used four pieces of paper and forty-five minutes to get the answer to the *first*. The answer was right, but I was doing it *my* way. One of my teachers eventually told me,

" 'You know, the way you do these problems is the same way they were done back in the nineteenth century.' "

Bill Cosby did not think too much of some members of the media—print or electronic—and there was good reason for it.

"Too many of these people would rather find out when

I was toilet trained than learn what I'm trying to do on a stage or on television."

Talk-show hosts and guests were always trying to get Cosby to talk about his "spiritual beliefs," and when they did so, he might respond something like this:

"The only way I can put it is, I don't have to go to a human being and have him tell me what Jesus said or what God said. I've made many, many mistakes in my life, and I will go on making many, many more. But I do believe that the best time is when your fellow human beings get a feeling from you and you get a feeling from them.

"Selfishness plays a large, large role in our lives, and many times we do things just to see if we can get away with it. The more power you have, the more you have to control yourself in terms of using and abusing people.

"I think that there is a Supreme Being, but I also think that it is our job to be as sensible as we can and not as selfish. Think twice and then go on with what you believe in."

Nevertheless most of them persisted in getting him to make statements about life as he sees it:

"I always wanted to survive," he told one writer. "I wrote on my wall years ago, 'I am too important to myself not to survive.'"

The Cosby philosophy, in a slightly tongue-in-cheek fashion, surfaces occasionally under the constant probing of journalists:

"In the beginning of my career I was idealistic. Now that I have things, someone is always there trying to take them away."

And, along the same lines, the Cosby personality expresses itself:

"I started out gregarious, but that part of me is being destroyed."

Akin to philosophy, of course, is religion. Cosby considers religion in his case to be a rather personal and individual thing, not particularly structured in the conventional fashion.

"I'm sort of a frightened atheist. If the sky were to open up tomorrow, I'd cop out. I'd probably try to con God. There are a few things I'd like to say to Him—but I don't think it can be done by prayer."

Sometimes he may simply avoid the question of religion by joking about it in a gentle, good-natured way:

"I was a very wicked child. I had a praying mantis that I converted to an agnostic."

In spite of this, Cosby keeps coming back to Bible stories again and again to make an important point about something.

"With all that physical space," he notes, "Cain and Able could have said, " 'All right, I'm going to take this side, and you take that side.'

"Instead, they stood there and hammered away at each other. Whenever I read that story, I think to myself, Well, that's man.

"But I've learned to balance that assessment, just as the Bible does, by thinking about some of the really fine people I've known. I guess my view of life is generally optimistic. I believe there are a lot of positive people around who want to take responsibility for their own lives. As long as we have those people, I'll be hopeful for the rest of us."

On an ABC-TV talk show Leeza Gibbons asked Cosby about how his children and family felt about his books. She was referring specifically to *Fatherhood*, a strong 1986 best-seller.

"Did they have any editorial rights on the book?" she asked him. "Did they say, 'Dad, I'll kill you if you put in the story about whatever'?"

Cosby was cautious. "Well, first of all my children would never mention killing me. But, of course, I *have* mentioned killing *them* once or twice. As a parent, that does come out of your mouth occasionally. It isn't true, but it's sort of like a curse word. It's from the viewpoint of the younger person you were—the one who thought all being a parent was going to be was to have them, give them truth, give them wisdom, give them love, support them spiritually, and then send them on to college—and then the wheels all come off!"

The Cosby kids came home one night and had no homework assigned them. This was a bit much for Bill Cosby. Let him tell it.

"I don't think there's such a concept as finished, not when it comes to education. So I told their teacher I wanted them to have homework because that's what will happen when they become professional people. There's always more to learn. That's what education is all about."

Cosby's thoughts return many times to his school days in Philadelphia, and particularly to Mary B. Forchic Nagle, the teacher who had Cosby in the sixth grade. She was the one teacher who made a great positive impression on him.

He always remembers the afternoon she took him downtown to a movie and to dinner.

"I was in the sixth grade and eleven or twelve years old before I even *saw* downtown Philadelphia. I was *so happy* to be downtown! After a movie [featuring Doris Day and Rock Hudson], my teacher took me to dinner and then she rode me home in a taxicab.

"This was a big thing, because in *my* neighborhood, if you rode in a taxicab, something bad—or something wonderful—had happened to you."

In his youth and in his adulthood Cosby has gambled, but not like a born loser. Nor did he ever let it get hold of him the way some wheeler-dealers do.

"I've never lost more than I could afford, never more than a half week's salary. In truth, I've often won more at the tables than what I was earning per week on stage!"

Skip Hinnant worked with Bill Cosby on the television series called *The Electric Company*. His impressions of Cosby were somewhat different from other people's.

"Bill was very open, very unpretentious. And he had the biggest collection of sneakers in the world! This was before running shoes became a fad. He'd come in with those leather sneaks or new tennis shoes and say, " 'Look at these, Skip, look at these!'

"And I'd want to go out and buy a pair, or he'd bring me a pair. That's all he ever wore—jeans and sneakers."

And Cosby was marvelous on the set, too. He was, according to Hinnant, "great fun." Also, he could be "very casual and funny." With all that, he had a great dignity. "You know you don't screw around with him, but at the same time you know you *can*."

Cosby continued to be dogged by members of the media and questioned about everything under the sun. They always seemed to be after something.

"I hate it when [magazine and newspaper] writers try to psychoanalyze my life. I mean, how many of them have degrees in psychiatry?"

Henry Silva, the actor, a good friend of Cosby's, called him on the telephone one day to inform him that Mrs. Silva was pregnant. To which Cosby responded joyfully:

"All right! Hey, hey, hey—put cotton in her shoes! Don't let her walk on the hard ground! All right! All right!"

Obsessed by the insistence of the media to pry into private affairs as well as professional affairs, Cosby finally got it all off his chest by saying:

"Well, I used to get really worried about what I was going to say during an interview, but I found out it never really matters. This guy who has never seen the sun wanders up to your hotel room. Maybe he is like Earl Wilson and he orders this floppy sandwich with a pickle. In between gulping down his free lunch it's 'gumble mulch gulp' for a question, and it doesn't matter what I say because he's going to write down what *he* thinks I should have said anyway."

"Mr. Cosby, what did you think about hanging up your stockings for Saint Nick to fill?" he was asked.

"Hell, when I was growing up we didn't have enough socks for our feet, let alone any spare ones to hang!"

"And what do you think about Christmas in general?"

"I'll tell you this—it shouldn't be all wrapped up in a fat guy in a red suit."

Cosby always came back to his beginnings. He remembered once when he was working in Philadelphia.

"When I was nineteen I was a shoe repairman's apprentice. Man, I thought that was *it*! . . . I stood at that window, hammering on shoes and looking out at the people waiting for the bus across the street, until I was going so crazy I started to *destroy* shoes. I loved putting two-inch heels instead of half-inch heels on some guy's shoes. Couldn't wait till he came to pick them up!"

On a talk show during the dead of night he got to chatting with his host about restaurants and barrooms and finally the talk went around to inebriates.

"You know, drunks never look down. They keep looking up and they stay like that because if they don't *do* like that and if they accidentally look *down*, they get dizzy from the height."

To Muriel Davidson, a *Good Housekeeping* writer, Cosby unburdened himself about some of the double standards we celebrate in this country.

"The national pastime in this country is not sex and it's not baseball. It's lying."

Cosby pointed out that the first thing a baby hears on this earth is someone saying,

"Oh, ain't that a beautiful baby!"

"Now, see," Cosby went on, "that baby *knows* he's not beautiful. He's wrinkled and bowlegged and slightly ugly. Right? So now the baby *knows* you're lying to him."

Then the proud parent takes the youngster to the doctor for the obligatory shots. And there's the *doctor* saying:

"This isn't going to hurt at all."

But the shots *do* hurt! It's *another* lie.

"More," Cosby continued. "The kid does something real bad." And so his father says to him, "God's going to punish you."

Cosby: "And there is this kid waiting for thunder and lightning and the plague—and nothing happens except he gets his bottom warmed by a very human hand. Another lie.

"And so now this poor, mixed-up kid doesn't even know whether he should believe in God anymore."

Cosby had other thoughts about lying. When he was in the sixth grade and he was talking with the rest of the kids about what they were all going to be when they grew up, one of Cosby's friends turned to him and laughed.

"Bill," he said, "you'd better plan on being either a lawyer or a performer."

"Why?" Cosby asked him, good straight man that he was.

"Because you lie so damned good!"

And there was always Russell and North Philly:

"I remember wanting to use the telephone once when I was growing up in North Philly. My brother, Russell, grabbed it ahead of me to call his girlfriend.

"Fifteen minutes later, I listened in and all I could hear was breathing. Picked it up in another ten minutes, and heard more breathing.

"Finally I yelled into the phone,

" 'I've got to use this phone!'

" 'You can't,' said my brother. 'We're talking.' "

He always had fun thinking back to his big-house and big-car days in Beverly Hills. For example, there was the problem he had with his twenty-four thousand dollar Rolls-Royce—a car that was supposed to be the best car ever made and totally trouble-free. Yes, without question there it was, ailing—

"It always ran so quiet, man, I didn't *know* it had broken down. But the trees weren't moving, so I figured it had. Then I figured maybe for the twenty-four thousand dollars I had paid for it, the place I was going to would come to me!"

But, you know, the place didn't—even for that expensive Rolls-Royce!

It was Mary B. Forchic (Nagle), Cosby's grade-school teacher, who perhaps summed up the essential Cosby in this statement made to his mother Anna about him:

"You have a fine son, one who should always stand out as a regular fellow, an excellent athlete, superb in dramatics, intellectual in all he does, and a mannerly boy."

And she was right, wasn't she?

CHAPTER ELEVEN

THE COSBY TRUTH

NOTHING CAN destroy the spontaneity of humor more readily than a serious analysis of it—nevertheless, the wit and fun in Bill Cosby are too important to be ignored and let go their ways without at least an attempt.

One Webster definition of humor includes the key phrase: "that quality which appeals to a sense of the ludicrous or absurdly incongruous." It is obvious that Noah Webster was no wit himself, and while there isn't really much meaning in the phrase of definition upon close inspection, it should serve as a springboard for a discussion of Cosby's sense of humor.

To underline an obvious point: The cartoonist uses sketches and drawings to evoke humor just as the standup comedian uses words and phrases. Cosby blends both the cartoonist's techniques of exaggeration and distortion with the standup comedian's facility with words and concepts.

Cosby himself knows what he is about. "You're a talking cartoonist," he has said about his own work, "painting images in the audience's head. If it sees the images as funny, then it laughs."

One of Cosby's most important talents is the ability to create Webster's "ludicrous" or "absurdly incongruous" images in the mind of the viewer, listener, or reader. He does it by using facial expressions, by using his voice in various ways, and by twisting his words about.

Take this example, in which Cosby talks about his football days at Temple University. After explaining that the coach used to hold what was called a "Who Was That?" clinic after each game, during which the entire team was forced to watch movies of the plays, he goes on:

"The coach stops the film and says, 'All right, who was that?' And then you have to stand up and the coach runs you down in Don Rickles fashion. Well, I was caught many times in 'Who Was That?' because I happened to be one of the few blacks on the squad, so it was very easy to pick me out. So the coach would say, 'Cosby, look at you. One hundred and eighty pounds of Jello. Jumping 'round, falling down, looking like somebody's chicken son.' My only answer to that was, 'Well, I'm never hurt.' "

The "image" of Cosby created by the words themselves is amusing—"jumping 'round, falling down, looking like somebody's chicken son."

Later he says, "I was always running down the sidelines as slow as I could go, trying to find a guy my weight so I could fall down in front of him."

To the basic idea of creating the incongruous image of a nonferocious ballplayer trying to *avoid* contact is added in this paragraph another of the humorist's favorite weapons: self-deprecation. Cosby paints himself as a coward in the midst of twenty-one other robust heroes. He's running *away*, not running *at* danger. Mixed in with self-deprecation is that most rare commodity—truth. And truth is another formidable weapon of the humorist.

There's a simple rule for a successful comedian: always maintain a balanced position and try to have a clear-eyed vision of life. Mark Twain wrote from common sense; it shines through in all his work. Will Rogers often commented on the fact that he got most of his laughs simply by telling the unvarnished truth!

The comedian either utilizes common sense to show someone else's absurd position, or to admit his own lack of it. For example, when Cosby signed on to do the television show *I Spy* in the 1960s, his wife, Camille, was expecting their first child. Cosby was so convinced that it was going to be a boy he prepared an ad to run in *Variety* as soon as the child was born.

The ad said: "I got the first man for my softball team." But the first Cosby child was a girl. He ran the ad anyway, adding at the bottom: "Oops! We'll treat her as if she was our son." As to the name for the first baby, Cosby wrote: "Haven't decided on the baby's name yet. Just gonna send him out to play, and whatever the kids call him, that's his name."

Note the twists and turns here. First, Cosby laughs at himself for the usual father's desire for a man-child. Second, he overrides common sense by ignoring the capriciousness of nature. Third, he immediately tries to rescue himself from the absurdity of his position by ignoring the facts and pretending the child is male anyway. The punchline is a twist on an old favorite, but nevertheless it works here with a double whammy, since there is the absurdity of letting the neighborhood name the child, combined with the continuing hypocrisy of claiming the daughter to be a son.

Logic, like common sense, can work just as well for a laugh. Here's Cosby on God and prayer:

"People shouldn't take God's name in vain, because He's so busy with Vietnam and the race questions, and by calling on Him they distract Him from His work. So I tell them I have a friend named Rudy who's not doing nothing and would be glad to help if they called on him. Just call on my friend Rudy when you want to make a point at the crap table.

" 'Oh, Rudy, please make me that hard eight!'

"You see?"

Cosby is a past master at working facial expressions,

body moves, and—most of all—unusual *sounds* to underline his jokes. This quip is funny in the reading, but it is even funnier when delivered by the inimitable Cosby voice:

"I got fed up with the football. I wanted to be a halfback, but I weighed a hundred and eighty-seven. They made me a fullback. There was no future in it. You go in through the middle of the line. You go through the guard slots. Every time: *PHBAM!*"

Cosby's forte actually is what might be termed "far-ranging characterization." He can throw himself into almost *any* role—the more incongruous the better—and come up with a laugh-provoking routine. His famed "karate school" skit starts out with his wisecrack about the number of karate schools in Greenwich Village—"twenty-three million!" Then he slips into the characterization of the karate graduate who feels so confident that he searches out dark alleys to saunter through with ten-dollar bills in plain sight to entice muggers. But the key laugh occurs when Cosby finds himself actually approached by a would-be attacker. He whirls, makes all the crazy moves of the karate master to demolish his attacker—but misses completely. Huh?

The mugger is a midget!

The key to the laugh here is the fact that it's a bonus. The main line of the story is funny in itself: The moves of the karate fighter are exaggerated mercilessly for effect. The shouts and grunts and snorts are perfect for Cosby's wide-ranging style of delivery. But of course at the end it all collapses into hysterical laughter as the defense fails because of the unexpected *size* of the assailant.

Cosby's "war" skits—he wasn't actually in combat—are based mostly on the self-deprecation concept: Cosby is the Rodney Dangerfield of the armed services, getting no respect at all—and for good reason. Once in the service, he becomes a medic. Then:

"I was very proud of it, because I read the Geneva Convention and it says you cannot shoot a medic."

Cosby then relates his experience in the front lines after cautiously settling down in a beach foxhole to "watch the war."

"And here's a guy next to me. A nut. When a buddy is shot, this nut runs out after him. And they [the enemy gunners] cut him down. First thing this guy says is: 'Medic!'

"I say, 'What do you want?'

" 'My leg! My leg!'

Pause.

" 'I don't make house calls.' "

It is always fun to see someone who is trapped in an impossible situation trying to work out of it. A good comedian spends enormous effort in setting up such a situation so as to be able to devise a wily and imaginative method of escape from it. Take Cosby:

He and his brother Russell have been fighting in their room and have broken the bed. Their father storms in:

FATHER: What's going on in here?
COSBY: A man came in through the window and started jumpin' on the bed until it broke.
FATHER: There's no window in this room.

Pause.

COSBY: He brought it with him!

Total absurdity—big laugh.

Here's another self-deprecatory remark as Cosby reminisces about his employment at the Gaslight Café in Greenwich Village: "The idea was to break the monotony of the folksingers. That was my job. In time, I became monotonous in my own right."

Incongruity comes in many forms. For example, there's a total impossibility in the concept of the time warp. Psychology calls this phenomenon the déjà vu: a situation in which you feel that you've been here *before* and heard or said the same thing *before*. In drama the reverse of this is called foreshadowing, preparing the audience for a later incident. But in Cosby's case it is the simple matter of an accidental prediction:

When he was in the sixth grade, his teacher became annoyed at him for clowning around during class and finally got up in front of them all and addresses Cosby:

"In this classroom there is *one* comedian and it is *I*. If you want to be one, grow up, get your own stage, and get paid for it."

And, of course, he did!

In addition to the time warp, there is also the incongruous situation of a word or phrase that means two or three different things and when used as an unintended double meaning can produce a laugh. This humorous device is cousin to the pun—the twisting about of a word or phrase that means two different things and when brought together produces an absurd image.

Playing the Lone Ranger's horse, Silver, Cosby looks over his shoulder in one skit and snarls at the famed Masked Rider: "Get off my back!"

Another Cosby standby is his use of memorable phrases and old wives' tales supposedly told him by his mother. The oft-quoted warning about the snakes around the crib is a typical one, printed earlier in chapter 8. Cosby frequently brings them up in his discussions of his early days in Philadelphia.

For example, here's a warning his mother used to voice when she saw him wolfing down grapes without spitting out the seeds:

"Eat grapes with the seeds in them and branches will grow out of your ears, and neighbors will hang clothes on your branches."

Obviously the image itself is enough for the laugh— Cosby as instant reindeer.

Kids are still the essence of Cosby's humor—his reminiscences of when he was young, his relationship with children today, and his thoughts about youngsters.

"I thought kids were the simplest little creatures in the world, once upon a time. That was before I had any of my own. But me, I'm someone who likes to do things in the overkill method. I had a kid—my wife helped, of course—and then another and another and . . . well, you get the picture."

Note how Cosby immediately brings the listener up short at the end of the first sentence—"once upon a time." He implies that he no longer thinks kids are simple. In the fourth sentence, he mocks the cliché statement of all fathers—"I had a kid"—by pointing out that, of course, his wife *did* help in a small way. Then, at the end of the paragraph, his thoughts stray from children to other more distracting considerations . . . and the laugh comes.

"It's the little things that count when you're a daddy," he says. "Like taking your little girl for ice cream. First you have to teach her about the concept of gravity. I can't tell you how many ice creams I've had to pick up off the floor, rinse off and stick back on my kid's cone. Now that may sound strange, but have you bought ice cream lately? Good gosh, it's up to seventy-five cents a scoop. A scoop! What's in it, gold? So you can't afford to lose a bit that dribbles down the sides; each dribble's worth maybe three cents."

Cosby mixes common sense with straight truth to achieve his laughs. The *image* of a kid with ice cream falling off the cone is funny in itself. Then, to comment on the *price* is a typical reaction of a cost-wise parent. Here the straight truth provides the laughter.

"If you listen carefully to what a child is saying to you, you'll see that he has a point to make. So I listen. And I answer them just as seriously as possible. And if I don't know the answer, I'll tell them I don't know."

Again, playing truth and straightforwardness, Cosby

relates how Sheldon Leonard, the producer of television's *I Spy,* was Cosby's Branch Rickey—the baseball manager who made Jackie Robinson the first black to play in the major leagues. "Everybody's always comparing me with Jackie Robinson," Cosby goes on, "but the thing of it is, you don't want to look at the first black doing a thing and say, 'Wow, boy!' It's the man who had the guts to *give* the break who really counts."

And that's Cosby's sense and sensibilities showing through; that's the Cosby *wit.*

"To get myself across and to be an important person, I made people laugh," he says. "Through humor, I gained acceptance."

And, on a more sober note, "What can young people, black and white, do to help improve relations? They can try to be as fair with each other as is humanly possible. That's the important thing: fair. Not what they think is fair, but what *is* fair."

In 1965, when Cosby was just beginning to gain fame as a nightclub comedian, Charles L. Mee Jr., an associate editor of the book division of American Heritage, wrote a piece for the *New York Times Magazine,* and made a prescient remark about him:

"There lurks, just over Cosby's shoulder, something more than a comedian, and one day that quality may fully emerge. He has the potential of a great clown, an artist who can conjure up his own world, bring it alive on stage and evoke from the audience that rare response to comedy: 'That's the truth. . . . That's a true story.' "

In Cosby's humor, one thing alone shines through—not the put-down, not the self-immolation, not the one-line play on words, but the plain, unvarnished truth.

He has said it himself:

"My one rule is to be true rather than funny."

BIBLIOGRAPHY FOR "THE COSBY WIT"

Newspapers and Periodicals

Atlas, Jacoba. "Bill Cosby and His Kids." PARENTS MAGAZINE (July 1978).

Bell, Joseph N. "Bill Cosby: Much More Than a Comedian!" GOOD HOUSEKEEPING (February 1980).

"Bill Cosby and Erika." SEVENTEEN (December 1978).

"Bill Cosby: 18 Years and a Lot of Laughs Later." TEEN (February 1986).

"Bill Cosby Remembers Phillie Joe." DOWNBEAT (December 1985).

"Bill Cosby's Number One Teacher." TODAY'S EDUCATION (October 1972).

Blinn, Johna. NEWSDAY (March 4, 1968).

"Call for Image Cleaning." TIME (April 28, 1986).

Capitol Records publicity handout on Bill Cosby (no date).

CHICAGO DAILY NEWS (July 25, 1964).

"Color Him Funny." NEWSWEEK (January 31, 1966).

Cosby, Bill. "Bill Cosby on Chicken Football." LOOK (November 4, 1969).

———. "Bill Cosby Talks about Middle Age and Other Aggravations." EBONY (December 1980).

121

———. "How to Win at Basketball: Cheat." LOOK (January 27, 1970).

DALLAS MORNING NEWS (March 18, 1985).

Darrach, Brad. "Cosby!" READERS DIGEST (September 1985).

Davidson, Bill. "I Must Be Doing Something Right." McCALLS (April 1985).

Davidson, Muriel. "Bill Cosby: The Man, His work, His Wife." GOOD HOUSEKEEPING (March 1970).

———. "Celebrating with the Bill Cosbys." GOOD HOUSE-KEEPING (December 1972).

———. "Command Performance." GOOD HOUSEKEEPING (March 1973).

"Day on the Town With Two Cosbys, A." SEVENTEEN (May 1982).

DiPetto, Adam. "Laughing on the Outside Too." NEW YORK DAILY NEWS (October 25, 1970).

Ebert, Alan. "Bill Cosby: A Piece of the Action." ESSENCE (December 1977).

Edwards, Audrey. "Bill Cosby's Two Wives; a Home with Camille Cosby." LADIES HOME JOURNAL (April 1986).

Feltman, Ann. "Laughing and Learning with Bill Cosby." PARENTS' MAGAZINE (September 1974).

Fury, Kathleen. "Witness the Humor of Bill Cosby." TV GUIDE (October 19, 1984).

Glenn, Larry. "Bill Cosby: The Clown as Straight Man." TUESDAY MAGAZINE (October 1956).

Gold, Todd. "Bill Cosby: The Doctor Is In." SATURDAY EVENING POST (April 1985).

Gussow, Mel. "Comedy: Bill Cosby Reflects on American Life." NEW YORK TIMES (February 3, 1986).

Haley, Alex. "Talking with Cosby." LADIES HOME JOURNAL (June 1985).

Hanauer, Joan. "Cosby at Harvard." United Press International (September 30, 1983).

Hemming, Roy. SENIOR SCHOLASTIC (March 18, 1965).

Henderson, Kathy. "Phylicia Ayers-Allen: Her TV Husband Married Her Off." REDBOOK (April 1986).

JERSEY RECORD (NJ) (April 26, 1974).

Johnson, Robert E. "TV's Top Mom and Dad." EBONY (February 1986).

Karnow, Stanley. "Bill Cosby: Variety Is the Life of Spies." SATURDAY EVENING POST (September 25, 1965).

Kasindorf, Jeanie. "Dr. Bill Cosby—a Laughing Matter?" NEW YORK (November 4, 1985).

Klein, Todd. "Bill Cosby: Prime Time's Favorite Father." SATURDAY EVENING POST (April 1986).

Lewis, Robert Warren. "Cosby Takes Over." TV GUIDE (October 4, 1969).

LIFE (March 15, 1968).

LIFE (April 11, 1969).

LOOK (May 30, 1967).

LOUISVILLE (KY) COURIER JOURNAL & TELEGRAM (March 26, 1972).

Mae, Charles L. Jr. "That's the Truth—and Other Cosby Stories." NEW YORK TIMES MAGAZINE (March 14, 1965).

NEWSWEEK (May 20, 1968).

NEWSWEEK (June 17, 1963).

NEW YORK DAILY NEWS (August 3, 1972).

NEW YORK DAILY NEWS (September 12, 1972).

NEW YORK POST (January 24, 1977).

NEW YORK TIMES (June 25, 1962).

NEW YORK TIMES (June 17, 1968).

O'Connor, John J. "Cosby in NBC Series on a New York Family." NEW YORK TIMES (September 20, 1984).

Oliver, Stephanie Stokes. "Parent-wise. A Father's Tribute: Bill Cosby Talks about Raising Children." ESSENCE (June 1984).

PACE (November 1964).

PHILADELPHIA BULLETIN (February 25, 1964).

Pierce, Ponchitta. "Bill Cosby—Laughter with Lesson." READERS DIGEST (August 1976).

Regan, Judith. "Bill Cosby's Two Wives; at Home with Clair Huxtable." LADIES HOME JOURNAL (April 1986).

Robinson, Louie. "Dr. Bill Cosby: He's a Comedian, Actor, Philosopher, Author, Educator, and Family Man." EBONY (June 1977).

———. "Pleasures and Problems of Being Bill Cosby." EBONY (July 1969).

SCHOLASTIC SENIOR (February 25, 1965).

Spina, James. WOMEN'S WEAR DAILY (no date).

Stang, JoAnne. "The Private world of Bill Cosby." GOOD HOUSEKEEPING (June 1967).

Townley, Roderick. "Phylicia Ayers-Allen: She'll Show You the Serenity—But Not the Strife." TV GUIDE (September 7, 1985).

Trott, William C. "People." United Press International (April 2, 1986).

Unger, Arthur. "Phylicia Ayers-Allen: Getting Beyond the Race Question. 'Cosby Show' Star Sees Acting as 'Touching People's Hearts.' " CHRISTIAN SCIENCE MONITOR (November 23, 1984).

VARIETY (March 12, 1969).

Washington, Mary Helen. "Please, Mr. Cosby, Build on Your Success." TV GUIDE (March 22, 1986).

Waters, Harry F. "Cosby's Fast Track." NEWSWEEK (September 2, 1985).

Waters, Harry F. and Peter McAlevey. "Bill Cosby Comes Home." NEWSWEEK (November 5, 1984).

Whitman, Arthur. "The Spy Who Knocked Him Cold." TRUE (January 1967).

Television Show Transcripts

CBS MORNING NEWS. WCBS/TV. May 27, May 28, 1986.

ENTERTAINMENT TONIGHT. WABC/TV. May 27, May 28, 1986.
HOUR MAGAZINE. WNYW/TV. May 26, May 27, and May 28, 1986.
MacNEIL/LEHRER NEWSHOUR. PBS/TV. December 28, 1984.
NIGHTWATCH, WCBS/TV. May 25, May 26, 1986.
PHIL DONAHUE SHOW. NBC/TV. May 26, 1986.
TONIGHT SHOW. WNBC/TV. June 13, 1986.
TONIGHT SHOW. WNBC/TV. Dates unknown.

Books

Berger, Phil. THE LAST LAUGH. New York: William Morrow & Company, 1975.
Cosby, Bill. BILL COSBY'S PERSONAL GUIDE TO TENNIS. B.Y.: Creative Education, 1974.
Ensor, Allison, MARK TWAIN & THE BIBLE. Lexington, Kentucky: University of Kentucky Press, 1969.
Latham, Caroline. BILL COSBY—FOR REAL. TOR Books, 1985.
MacDonald, J. Fred. BLACK AND WHITE TV. Chicago: Nelson & Hall Publishers, 1983.
Neider, Charles, ed. THE COMPLETE ESSAYS OF MARK TWAIN. Garden City, New York: Doubleday & Company, 1963.
Olsen, James T. BILL COSBY: LOOK BACK IN LAUGHTER. N.Y.: Creative Education, 1974.
Smith, Ronald L. "COSBY!" New York: St. Martin's Press, 1986.
Woods, Harold and Geraldine. BILL COSBY: MAKING AMERICA LAUGH AND LEARN. Minneapolis, Minn.: Dillon Press, Inc., 1983.

Reference

CONTEMPORARY BIOGRAPHY.
WHO'S WHO.